Choosing to See Beauty

*My Story of Moving Past
Trauma and Mental Illness*

MAURA PRESZLER

CATHOLICPSYCH
PRESS

Cover and book design by Anna Guerin, annamicheledesigns.com. Image by Hannah Quintana Photography.

Dedication

Michael, you are one of the greatest gifts God the Father has blessed me with. Thank you for loving me in my brokenness. You have never seen my past as a burden, and this is a testimony to your compassionate and gentle heart. My heart beats for you.

Clare, thank you for sitting with me during some of my greatest pain. Your empathy and love for others is unparalleled. I love you deeply.

Note to the Reader

The stories in this book reflect the author's recollection of events. Some names, locations, and identifying characteristics have been changed to protect the privacy of those depicted. Dialogue has been re-created from memory.

Table of Contents

Introduction

My story is not an easy one to write. I saw and experienced things as a child that no one should ever have to. I have lived so much of my life in a chronic state of anxiety, depression and fear. Reflecting on my journey of healing and recovery, I know that I am alive and thriving today by the grace of God, therapy, medication, exercise, hard work and perseverance. I share my story so God may be glorified through my words. I truly believe in the power of stories and it is my hope that God will use my story to inspire you in your journey.

People need other people and I hope my story helps you to know that you aren't alone. Throughout my journey of healing, many people have shared their stories with me and it was through their vulnerability that a large part of my healing took place because it gave me permission to use my voice, to tell my story, to go to therapy and find healing.

I share my story not to shame or blame my family or anyone involved but to hopefully instill hope in our broken world. I've held onto this manuscript for many years and my three little sons, Pio, Noah and Luke have inspired me to finally publish it.

When I look at their innocence, I am reminded that there is so much beauty in our broken world. Learning to see beauty in my brokenness has been a journey for me, a journey of tremendous pain but also a journey of so much goodness. My sons remind me daily to continue to strive to live a life of gratitude and I am exceedingly grateful for all that God the Father has done for me.

CHAPTER 1

The Beginning

When I was twenty-four, I completed extensive psychological testing at the Institute for the Psychological Sciences (IPS), in Arlington, Virginia. During one of the tests, the doctor asked me to draw a picture of the house I grew up in. Filled with apprehension, I did as she said. After I drew the picture, she asked, "If these walls could talk, what would they say?"

Oh my gosh, this is so dumb, I thought, giving her a blank stare.

"Just take a moment to think about it, Maura."

Seconds turned to minutes as we sat there together in silence. I could hear the clock ticking as she probed again, "What do you think?" I remember trying so hard to be tough, but my eyes flooded with tears that I desperately tried to hold back and that trickled down onto the picture. *They would say they have seen so much violence, and some good times.*

I would like to start my story with the *good times* those walls saw.

One Sunday morning I woke up, looked out my window, and saw my dad walking around the cul-de-sac in front of our house. I knew he was cooling down after his run. In an impulse reaction, I jumped out of bed. My little feet hit the cold, hard wood floor of my bedroom, and I raced down the hallway through a maze of laundry and down the stairs to meet my dad at the back door.

"Can you teach me to run?" I begged.

That afternoon my dad took me to Sports Authority to get a pair of running shoes. As I walked down the kids' shoe aisle, I remember being in awe that I was going to be a runner just like my dad and that I was at the store without any of my siblings. Being the fourth of seven children, an outing alone with either parent was rare.

My dad reached up, took down a box, and handed it to me. I knew what was inside, but instantaneously I became shy, like a young child mesmerized by Santa Claus who when the time actually comes to sit on his lap, becomes hesitant.

I gently pulled back the tissue paper in the shoebox to reveal a pair of light purple running shoes that were just my size. I beamed with pride, thinking, *Now I can run with my dad*. I was five years old.

My dad grew up across the street from the Atlantic Ocean. He could stand in his bedroom and see the waves curl, crash, and wash up on the beach, along with watching the sun rise every morning. He could hear the seagulls squawking and the resultant sounds of dropping clamshells on his roof, driveway, or decks as they cracked them open to eat what was inside. At night he could hear the waves crashing along the shore as he drifted off to sleep, and if he left his window open, he could smell the salt air drifting off the ocean and permeating his room.

Where he lived, they had a boardwalk built by the Works Progress Administration during the Great Depression in the 1930s. A boardwalk consists of boards laid horizontally about fifteen feet wide on the top of the sand and parallel to the Atlantic. It was here that my dad began his running career. At that time, running was not all popular in America, and those that ran were considered loners and misfits.

The street I grew up on was a runner's dream. There was a cul-de-sac on one end, with a dead end on the either end of the street, and the loop was six-tenth of a mile. Our house was in the middle of the loop, high on a hill. The cul-de-sac in front of our house was perfect for sports, and my six siblings and I definitely put it to good use.

The neighborhood children loved when we came out to play because in an instant we could make a sports team. I spent countless hours of my childhood playing in that cul-de-sac. It's where I learned to ride my bike, play tennis, roller hockey, kickball, baseball, and even parallel park years later.

That first fall Sunday evening when I went running for the first time is one of my favorite childhood memories. As my dad and I walked down our driveway, he said we could run one loop.

"Do you think you are up to that?" he asked.

"Just one loop?" I asked. "Why not two? I can do it." Two loops definitely sounded better than one, and after all, I was a runner now and had the shoes to prove it. My dad said one loop was good and that I was too young for anything more than that just now.

The air was crisp, and I could feel the wind against my face. It was dusk, so our shadows were dim, and the stillness of the night was so peaceful to my little mind. As we neared the end of the loop my dad said we could race to the driveway, so I pumped my little arms faster and put a little extra effort into my stride. My dad extended his stride as well, but I was determined to get to the driveway first. I didn't know it then, but of course he let me win. My naive five-year old self, though, thought I had just beaten a grown man. My dad gave me a high-five after we reached the driveway, and I smiled.

It wasn't long before I started racing. My first race was The Great Race in Middletown, New Jersey. The night before the race, I could barely sleep, I was so excited. My dad parked our car about a half mile from the race's festivities, so we walked there. As we got closer, I could see the track, and the field in the middle was full of sponsors. I didn't know what to expect, but I remember it being better than I imagined. With butterflies in my stomach, I reached up to tug on my dad's sleeve to get his attention.

"Is that where we finish?" I asked, pointing to the track. He nodded.

When we reached the middle of the field, we stood in line to pick up our race packets. When I got mine, I reached my little hand inside to pull out my race number. While my dad safety pinned my number to my shirt, I asked if I could wear the shirt inside my race bag for the race.

"Real runners don't ever wear their race shirt during the race," he responded.

"Why?" I asked inquisitively.

"Because that's something a first-time racer would do."

"But I am a first-time racer."

He looked at me and smiled. "You can put it on after the race."

When it was time, we walked over to the startling line. I thought the nerves in my stomach were going to explode.

"Don't leave me," I said to my dad. He reassured me that we were running the race together and that he wouldn't leave my side.

"You ready?" he said.

"I'm ready."

The gun was fired and with it my nerves. I exploded with energy and ran faster than I had ever run before. My dad stayed with me the whole time as promised. My favorite part about the race was his confidence in me and how it felt when we neared the finish line. My dad leaned down and said, "Let's really race to the end."

I didn't think I could run any faster, but somehow I managed to move my skinny legs faster. We crossed the finish line together, and he gave me a high-five and a hug.

I won a little trophy and carried it with tremendous pride. We walked toward the middle of the field where all of the sponsors were. There was a firetruck, an ambulance, and so many food vendors. My dad said it was important to drink, so I did. Then I had some orange slices and ice cream.

Since The Great Race was my first race, its ambiance is what I compared so many future races to. Sadly for me, this was one of the few races that served ice cream, and I often wondered why. That race gave me an even greater resolve to be a runner, and my dad and I would run many races together over the years.

As the years passed, my parents started letting me run by myself on our street, and I loved the freedom. I played other sports throughout my childhood, but nothing compared to running. Over time I got used to the standard running jokes that people, mainly my brothers, would taunt me with. They would always say that running wasn't really a sport and that it didn't require any hand-eye coordination. It bothered me, and I was convinced that they would love running if they gave it a try. Ironically, my two older brothers are runners today.

My love for the outdoors comes from my dad. Another memory of beauty and a highlight of my summer was when he would take some of my siblings and me camping. Our favorite place to go camping was Lake Champlain, which is located between New York and Vermont. Its fresh water stretches to the Canadian providence of Quebec, and the view is majestic. My dad bought two forest-green expedition canoes for our adventures. We named one *The James Caird*, which was the name of Sir Ernest Shackleton's boat during his 1914–1916 Endurance expedition. The other canoe we named *Indefatigable* after one of Horatio Hornblower's ships. We called it *Indy* for short.

Growing up, we had a fifteen-passenger van, because there were so many of us, and we needed a few extra seats in the car for friends. It was nice to have a little extra room for long trips too. Our tan Ford van might not have gotten the best gas mileage, but it was great for transporting our expedition canoes. We would hoist them on top of the car and strap them down securely.

We each had a dry bag for our camping trips that we pack with a sleeping bag, a few clothes, towels, and anything else we might need for the journey. We had a communal dry bag for all of our mess kits and food, and one more for miscellaneous items such as matches and lanterns. Everything we didn't want to get wet had to go in a dry bag in case we capsized, which we never did. We put our fishing poles and tackle boxes at our feet.

From our home in New Jersey, it was roughly a seven-hour drive to Lake Champlain. It was a beautiful drive through the country, and the mountains in the background made the view picturesque. When we arrived, we lifted the canoes off the van and carried them, our dry bags, and our fishing equipment down to the shoreline.

From the shoreline to the center of the island, it was a two-and-a-half-mile canoe paddle. There were five campsites on the island, with at least a half mile in between each one. I loved when my dad was able to rent the campground on the tip of the island. This particular campsite had the best excess to the water, a breathtaking view, and the most open space.

When we arrived at our campsite, we had to work quickly because dusk was almost upon us. We set up our tents, started a fire, unpacked our supplies, and two of us went out in one of the canoes for water.

We spent our days fishing, exploring, hiking, running, and swimming. We always managed to find the most dangerous things to do when my dad was back at the campground, which in my young mind equaled the most fun. We would pack a lunch of a power bar, dried fruit, and nuts and head out for a day of exploration, imagining we were a part of Sir Ernest Shackleton's pathfinders. One of my favorite things to do was go fishing at dusk. My brother Brian and I were always the loudest, and my dad used to say that we scared the fish away with our jokes and laughter.

These memories hold a special place in my heart and make me think of my dad in a positive light. If I only focused on the abuse and incredible dysfunction in my family, I would have drowned in my own pain. The happy times with my dad, even though they were mixed with confusion and anxiety because I never knew when he might get mad or my parents were going to fight helped me to have some semblance of order in my volatile childhood. The better memories also remind me that there is goodness in all of us, even when sometimes it's difficult to see the good in another. Reminiscing on these happier times growing up makes me wish I could have a real conversation with my dad and tell him that I only desire his good and that I hope he finds peace and healing in his life. I wish I could tell him that I hope we are in Heaven together one day.

If I could speak freely to him right now, I would tell him that I know he tried and that I'm so very sorry for his pain. Abuse is generational and therefore a learned behavior, so I know he learned it from someone who was supposed to show him love, affection, and direction. I would give him a hug and let him cry because I know the pain can be so deep at times and I can't imagine holding it inside for all those years. I would tell him that God the Father loves him and desires freedom for him for all the shame and guilt he carries. I would tell him he is a beloved son of God.

I would tell him how much I desperately wanted a father growing up. I would tell him how much therapy helped me and that I wish he would try it. I would tell him that I forgive him for the immense pain and suffering he caused. I would tell him about my loving and compassionate husband, Michael, and how sad it was that he missed our wedding. I would tell him about our precious little boys and how it saddens me that he won't know them like Michael's dad does. I would tell him that even though he caused a tremendous amount of damage and hurt in my life, God's grace is stronger than abuse. And that because of the abuse, I know God the Father, and my relationship with Him is the greatest gift in my life. I would tell him what it's like to know a loving Father, because I believe his heart yearns for that love. I would tell him that he has what it takes and that it's never too late to make amends.

CHAPTER 2

My Battle with Food

Growing up, I experienced so much confusion in the home I was raised in. I know my dad desired to be a present and good father to us; he just didn't know how. He was the first dad in the pool swimming with us at night—or he would punish us by not going to the pool at all. He would play this game we called Bears in the Basement on good nights. We would turn all the lights off and he would blindfold himself, get on his hands and knees and try to find us and then tickle us. He read many books to my siblings and me too. The source of my confusion was his extreme behaviors. He was present one night and abusive the next. I didn't understand it, and I remember being crippled with anxiety, but I didn't know what to call those feelings.

When my parents were fighting, I would shudder upon hearing the garage door open in the evening when my dad came home. *Would he be mad? Had I done something wrong? Were my parents going to fight all night?* Thinking about what might happen after dinner made me sick to my stomach with nervousness.

Would the police come that night? Would my mom lie again and tell the police officers she had fallen?

When I heard her do that, I wanted to scream. I wanted to tell the whole world that she hadn't fallen again, but instead my dad almost killed her. I saw his hands wrapped around her neck. I saw the knife. I saw her gasping for air. I knew the pain well, because it happened to me too.

Would I be brave enough to tell the police what was really going on?

So much of growing up was like walking on eggshells. I never knew what to accept.

Why would she let him do that to me? Didn't she love me enough to protect me? Would my dad be there? Would he leave? Would he, in his rage, smash the dishes to the floor? Would he destroy my artwork? Would he tell me, yet again, that I was worthless?

I grew accustomed to my dad's derogatory remarks. And over time, I began to believe them—that was the sad part. I really believed that I was worthless and would never amount to anything.

At the very core of my being, all my heart ached for was a father. A father to protect me. A father to comfort me when I had nightmares instead of giving them to me. A father to tell me I was beautiful. A father to teach me to dance. A father to hold my hand in the rain. A father to give me a hug before bed.

All of the anxiety I experienced carried over into my relationship with food.

I remember the first time I had anxiety about food. When my parents fought and my dad got violent, my mom would often take us out to dinner. We would go to Charlie Brown's, which serves American food. If my parents weren't fighting, we would rarely go out to eat, because our family was so large, and it was expensive. So while in my mind going out to eat was considered a treat, when my parents were fighting, it wasn't a treat because I was filled with fear. The whole situation left me very confused.

I would always order the hamburger from the kids' menu. It came with all you could eat from the salad bar, which I loved. I didn't even know what a calorie was at the time, but when my food came, I remember feeling sick to my stomach just looking at it. I was riddled with anxiety and felt like I had something stuck in my stomach. I was worried about my parents. I hated the fighting, and I hated the unknown of what the night might bring.

Two months before graduating from eighth grade, while warming up before field hockey practice, I overheard two high school girls gossiping about a girl in my class who had a heavier build than I. *Why are they speaking about her like that? That's so cruel!* I thought. My mind began to race. *I wonder if they talk about me like that? What if they laugh about me and think I'm fat too?*

I glanced down at my scuffed-up oxford shoes and noticed my skirt, which was supposedly two inches too short for the school. Every morning one of the teachers reminded me, "Maura, your skirt is too short. Please tell your mom to fix it, or you will need to get a new one."

Now I panicked. *Great, now people are going to talk about me because I'm fat and my skirt is too short.* I was an exceedingly anxious child, and when corrected or talked to harshly, I shattered.

Upon arriving home from school later that day, I told my mother that I wasn't going to be eating desserts again. My mother just looked at me, perplexed. After all, what normal child says such things? *Well, I'm going to show them that I'm not kidding. I'm going to start running and swimming more and eating less. I'll prove it.*

I was one of the thinnest girls in my class and had been a runner since I was five years old, so naturally my weight was never something I needed to even remotely worry about. But that night I stared intently in the mirror and decided that if I was going to be considered beautiful, I needed to lose weight. All I could hear was the mirror shouting at me: "Beautiful girls are thin, and you're ugly."

My mom insisted that I eat breakfast before school, so I started purposely getting up later so I wouldn't have time. I promised her I would eat my waffles as I walked to the bus stop.

But I lied.

Every morning I tossed the waffles down the sewer as I approached the bus stop. *I have to do this because no one believes that I need to lose weight. What are they thinking? Why don't they see how fat I am?* In my mind, this is how I justified the lies.

As the weeks passed, the lies started darting out of my mouth daily, and the person I was becoming frightened me.

"Oh, I already ate breakfast, Mom."

"Yes, lunch was delicious—thanks, Mom."

"I had a snack on the bus. I'm not hungry."

"I only ran five miles" (when I had actually run eight).

"See, Mom, I ate lunch, and there's my dish in the sink to prove it." (I had really just taken a clean dish from the cabinet, crumbled up some bread so it looked like I had eaten, and placed it in the sink.)

I weighed myself twenty times a day. I allowed myself between 100 and 200 calories a day. If I survived the day on 100 calories, I considered it to be a good day. If I had overeaten, which meant 300 calories, I made sure to punish myself the next day by running more miles and eating even more meager portions. I went to bed starving, and most nights I couldn't sleep because my hunger pains kept me awake. My body ached.

Why is it that my friends could eat pizza, then ice cream, and wake up the next morning and eat breakfast without worrying about their weight? Plus, they don't even exercise. I mean, come on, what is up with that? And here I am eating next to nothing and exercising daily, and I still feel fat. What is wrong with me? Will I ever be free from these thoughts that plague me constantly? Will I ever be able to enjoy food again? Will I ever be able to eat like I used to and not think of myself as fat? Will I ever be able to run in moderation? Will I ever be normal again? I just want to eat a piece of greasy pizza so badly and have a big bowl of Ben & Jerry's Chunky Monkey ice cream.

I shunned every reflection of myself, whether that was in a mirror, window, pane of glass, or the pool. When I saw myself, I shuddered. *Ah, I'm so ugly. I can't even stand the sight of myself. How do people even look at me?*

I had a pair of khaki J. Crew pants that I would try on multiple times throughout the day. Those pants defined me. They were literally my lifeline. If I felt like I had eaten too much or gained weight, I would immediately try those pants on. *Ah, they are too tight! Okay, I need to lose weight and run more.* Or, *Phew, they are still loose. Okay, I can relax for an hour or two.* I was a slave to those pants for years.

When the doctor told me that I would still be considered *thin* if I gained thirty pounds, I nearly passed out. *Thirty pounds? Are you crazy? I would explode if I gained ten pounds! I wouldn't be able to fit through the door or sit in a normal seat on an airplane, let alone look at myself if I gained thirty pounds. Gross! I'm already ugly enough. Why does she want me to be a whale? Maybe because she is overweight herself? Yes, that's got to be it, she doesn't want anyone to be thin because she's fat. This doctor is crazy!*

My parents fighting and the abuse in my life plagued me. I didn't know it at the time, but my eating disorder was all that I could control. I didn't think I was worth three meals a day. I was terrified that if I started eating again, I wouldn't have the self-control to stop. I convinced myself that it was better not to eat breakfast—because what if I couldn't stop and just kept eating and blew up to three hundred pounds overnight? I was afraid that if I stopped running fifty plus miles a week, I would *let myself go*.

Several weeks later as I was lying in bed starving, I could literally hear my heart struggling to beat. I was petrified. I took my pulse, and it was in the high twenties. I fought back tears because I was afraid my heart wouldn't be capable of handling the energy my tears would produce.

My bones were protruding. I was freezing in ninety-degree weather. My hair was falling out in clumps. My fingernails were purple, and I had fine hair growing all over my body. I knew that I had to make a change, or I could die. I reached for my rosary beads and started praying as a matter of habit. I promised God that if I was alive the next morning, I would try to get better and one day be an advocate for women in their recovery.

After I finished praying the Rosary, I realized that I was missing out on life. I wasn't allowed to go to dance class anymore, compete on the swim team, run, or go to summer camp. Not being able to go to summer camp crushed me. Yes, I was breathing, but I wasn't living. I was simply surviving, hoping that tomorrow I would still fit into my J. Crew pants. I was miserable.

I wanted to be healthy.

I yearned to enjoy my life minus counting calories. I daydreamed about what it would feel like to eat a bowl of ice cream without worrying about the caloric intake. I wanted to put half-and-half in my coffee like a normal human being. I wanted to lick the bowl after making brownies and not obsess over the fat content in the chocolate and butter. I wanted to drink orange juice again. I wanted to live!

Recovering from an eating disorder is a lifelong journey, and I am still growing today. The healing phase was excruciating and definitely not a quick fix. Years later when I went to therapy and learned about my dignity and worth, I removed the towels I had put over my bathroom mirror. Over time, I was gradually able to glance in the mirror without cringing. For the first time in years, I didn't see an ugly human being anymore.

I learned that seeing my ideal number on a scale would never fulfill me. It's exceedingly empty and tiring. And trust me, I tried everything. At my lowest weight, I was ninety-five pounds and five feet, eight inches tall. Instead of dwelling on what I disliked about my body, I tried to focus on what I liked. I wrote a list in my therapy journal and here is what it said:

I love my long hair. I love my big blue eyes. I love that I have long legs. I love my cheekbones.

I love that I'm athletic and like to run. I love that I can create things with my hands. I love that I can swim in the ocean and know how to ride the waves.

It's interesting—I have one dimple on the right side of my face. I wonder why I don't have them on both sides. Anyway, I use to hate that dimple, but then a guy I went on a date with told me it was cute. It's growing on me. I don't love it yet, but I'm getting there.

I love my resilient attitude.

I pondered how much physical exertion it took to exercise without any fuel in my body. Or how many hours I spent planning my "meals," which were more like small snacks. I pondered the days I wasted obsessing over counting calories, keeping my eating disorder a secret, and the relationships my eating disorder strained.

What would happen if I put all of the energy that I use to keep my eating disorder alive toward recovery? I would be a changed person; I'm sure of it. I know it would hurt. But on the flip side, I can't live like this forever. Let's be real: I'm miserable. I'm destroying relationships and slowly killing myself. I want to live again.

I tried to remember that just because I had a moment of struggle, defeat, or a bad day in my journey of recovery, it didn't mean that I hadn't made progress toward freedom.

I actively worked on being patient with myself and taking one step at a time. I sought to embrace change, and when I fell, which I did, I didn't stay down. Instead, I dusted off the dirt and tried to embrace each opportunity in my life to seek beauty. I started anew the next day, and no matter how many times I messed up, I never gave up.

I learned that recovering from my eating disorder isn't about being perfect. It was about making smart daily choices, even if

I didn't feel like it. Those daily choices eventually helped me to form new habits, which cultivated a lifestyle change.

In the beginning of my recovery, it was an intense challenge for me to put a spoon or fork in my mouth. I felt like I was shoving food down my throat. So, in the beginning I had to eat with my fingers, forcing myself to stay at the table until I had eaten a serving of food. Eventually I started using utensils again. Today I can eat a bowl of ice cream at one o'clock in the morning and not give it a second thought. I drink orange juice now and put half-and-half in my coffee. I can go out to dinner at a restaurant or to my favorite coffee shop and get a mocha and not obsess over the caloric content. I work out in moderation, and I never run over three miles anymore.

It's been over twenty years since eighth grade, and reflecting on my journey, I have learned that my validation of beauty and sense of acceptance isn't the width of my waist or my BMI. I can never quench my yearning to be loved through the number that flashes back at me on the scale. My worth comes from my intrinsic dignity as a daughter of God.

CHAPTER 3

Days of Anxiety

One night while I was in eighth grade, I called the police because my dad was being so violent and abusive. As I ran toward the phone and dialed 911, my dad charged at me, disconnected the phone, and threw me to the ground. The call had already gone through, and two police cars showed up at our house ten minutes later. The anxiety I felt and the pit in my stomach is a feeling I can still remember to this day. The police took my dad that night, and I was so relieved he was gone.

My mom never let us go outside without our shoes on, but at 1:00 a.m. that night, I walked barefoot in our front yard and caught fireflies. I came inside, walked into the kitchen, and cut my feet on all the broken dishes and glass on the floor. I wanted to clean it all up, but my mom told me to go to bed. I didn't sleep at all that night. I was so anxious I thought I was going to pass out.

The next day at school, during science class I told my teacher I had to go to the bathroom. Instead I headed toward the principal's office. I wanted to tell the principal what was going on at home, but when I got to his office that afternoon, I froze in fear. I couldn't articulate a string of words. I thought about just screaming "Help!" but couldn't get the words out. It took me over ten years to forgive myself for not telling him.

I was homeschooled in high school and hated it. I was so angry at my parents for taking me out of school. Going to school was a getaway for me. I loved the teachers and my friends, and I enjoyed learning. I felt safe there.

One of the harshest things my dad ever said to me was something that should never be vocalized, and yet surprisingly it's something many people tell themselves frequently. I remember that day, even though with time, its cruelty has faded, like the sun disappearing over the ocean at sunset. I was twelve, with short brown hair. I even remember the floral shirt I was wearing; its brightly colored flowers were just about the happiest thing I would gaze at that day. We were on a winding staircase, and the walls were lightly coated in a dusty sand color. The ceiling was high, and I could see the cobwebs above. But things like spiders didn't scare me. I thought it silly to jump at the sight of a bug the way other girls did.

I was different from other girls my age. Life aged me quickly, and I couldn't relate to most of the things the girls talked about at school. While they were worried about their hair, clothes, and boys, I was just trying to survive another day. And the sad part was that no one knew what I was going through. I wanted to tell someone so badly, but I feared no one would believe me.

The staircase had many steps. My father's face was so close to mine that I could taste his spit. At that moment I wished that for just ten seconds time would stand still so I could smack him as hard as my young hand could. But since I knew that would never happen, I held my rage inside. He was fuming. *You've touched me for the last time*, I thought. Every time was the last time in my mind, but in reality, it wasn't.

His tempering was raging. "You'll never amount to anything!" he screamed. "It would have been better off if you had never been born."

My heart froze.

Even then, for a second, I craved his affection. *Why did he hate me so?* His words sliced my heart wide open. The emotional pain hurt more than the time he threw me through a door so hard it broke and my body pounded into a cement block.

Time passed and I went to college. On the last day of the semester, when I handed in my final project to my professor, he wished me a Merry Christmas and asked if I had a moment.

"Of course," I said, nodding and secretly fearing the worst.

"You're one of the hardest working students I've ever taught," he said, "and with your attitude, discipline, and work ethic, you will go far in life. Keep up the good work. It was a pleasure to teach a student like you. See you next semester."

My face turned bright red. Not being accustomed to praise, I was shocked. My father's words from long ago came to mind. "You'll never amount to anything! It would have been better off if you had never been born."

I could go far in life? This was new to me. My father was wrong. At first it was as if his cruel words fueled me to prove him wrong. And in a way my professor's words just had. But it was my hard work and God's grace that cultivated those words. I don't say that in a prideful way—on the contrary, I was taken back that my professor thought that of me but proud that I hadn't listened to my father.

It took years, but I have forgiven my father. In fact, I'm grateful. Please don't misinterpret—I would never wish any sort of abuse on anyone. But the only way to navigate through the sufferings of life is to focus on the positive, to be grateful for what you do have instead of dwelling on what you don't. To try, with God's grace, to see beauty in your suffering, to navigate through the muck, rise from the ashes, and inspire others to do the same. This is our calling in life; this is our mission.

The truth is, I didn't amount to something because I was successful in school or had a successful job. I amounted to something before I was even born. I amounted to something because I'm a daughter of God, created in the image and likeness of Love Himself. I'm created with a purpose—out of love and for love. I'm enough simply because I'm His daughter. It took me years to learn this truth, and I'm still discovering God's goodness.

I spend time with God every day because I truly am nothing without Him, and His grace aids me in seeing beauty in my suffering and in constantly being reminded of all that He has done and continues to do for me. I often think about what it will be like to see our Heavenly Father face-to-face.

CHAPTER 4

College Days

My freshman year of college, I went to the College of Saint Elizabeth in Morristown, New Jersey. I was disappointed that they didn't have a cross country team, but I was awarded a good scholarship, so I accepted. I really wanted to make their soccer team, so I went to Sports Authority one afternoon and bought twenty-five soccer balls. Every morning that summer before my classes, I went for a run and then went to practice my soccer skills at a nearby soccer field before work. I would kick the balls to one end of the field and then the other for two hours each day. I was determined to make the soccer team, and I did.

My sophomore year of college, I transferred to Seton Hall University in South Orange, New Jersey, to be with my sister Clare. I walked on to their Division 1 cross-country team. Being a student athlete was challenging, especially with my issues with food and weight. I was really struggling with binge eating, and looking back I don't even know how I was able to run the distances and times I did. As athletes we were being weighed constantly and having our BMI taken, and this was so hard for me. I was always comparing my weight to the other girls on the team. I was constantly trying to be thinner but because I was bingeing so much, I was only gaining weight. Sometimes I still wonder how much differently my student-athlete experience would have been if I hadn't struggled with eating so much.

Many of my friends were involved with FOCUS (Fellowship of Catholic University Students), and they continually encouraged me to attend one of the missionaries' Bible studies or one of their own studies. Each time they invited me, I came up with another excuse as to why I couldn't make it. I continually thought, *I don't do Bible studies*, as if I were too good to attend a Bible study. Who was I kidding? I kept Jesus at arm's length. I did go to daily Mass often because it was the only place that I felt any peace in my heart.

I was afraid of getting too intimate with God, though, for fear of what He might ask. My thought process went something like this: *Well, I'm most definitely not becoming a nun, so there is no need for me to do a Bible study*, as if going to a Bible study meant that I was entering the convent. Laughable, I know.

Despite my ignorant thoughts, God still pursued me. He knew how much Varsity Catholic would touch my heart. He continued to offer me chances to accept an invitation to a Bible study, through my friends and the FOCUS missionaries that invited me. Each time they sought me out, I thought, *Do these people ever give up? I said no already.*

During my junior year of college, I met Amanda. She was a first-year missionary helping to start Varsity Catholic at Seton Hall. Amanda graduated from the University of Illinois in 2007 with a degree in Material Science Engineering. She declined a prestigious job offer to answer God's call to serve His Church as a missionary with FOCUS.

I was injured about a month into our cross-country season that year, and that's how God used Amanda to reach me and show me the love of the Father in a radical way. While doing a pool workout with my coach, I saw Amanda at the other end of the pool doing laps by herself. When my coach gave me a five-minute break at the side of the pool, Amanda approached me. "Hey girl," she said, "I'm going to start a Bible study for athletes, and I would love to have you come."

I silently thought, *What is up with these FOCUS people and their Bible studies? I don't do Bible studies, and I've said it a million times. Why won't they leave me alone?*

I forget what she said next, but there was something different about Amanda that I couldn't identify at the moment, and I liked being around her. Maybe it was the fact that I had never been asked to join a Bible study at the side of a pool. *Wouldn't outside of church be better for this sort of thing?* Or maybe it was her voice, personality, or the interior peace she possessed. Whatever it was that Amanda had, I wanted. So I just blurted out, "Okay."

She said she would email me a list of dates and times after she spoke with some of the other female athletes. My coach signaled to me that my five minutes was up, and I put my goggles back on. As I glided through the water, all I could think was, *How the heck am I going to get out of this one?*

I dried off after swimming and walked out of the recreation center. As the cold air hit my face, I pondered, *Why am I so afraid to go to a Bible study? I go to daily Mass, but I don't want to go to Bible study—it doesn't make sense, does it?*

I had built up so many walls, and I didn't want to break them down because I was scared about what might be on the other side. God knew this and used Amanda to gently break down a wall that evening.

When I received Amanda's email about Bible study the following week, I thought, *Well, there is still time to get out of this.* At the same time, there was a part of me that was tired of all the excuses, and Amanda intrigued me. When the night for our first Bible study came, I packed my Bible in my backpack and walked over to the cafeteria from the library. I was actually slightly surprised at myself and thought as I walked into the cafeteria, *I guess I'm really doing this.*

The Bible study was held in the glass atrium attached to the cafeteria. As I passed by the last food station before arriving at the atrium, there was a little voice inside my head that screamed out, *There is still time to turn around and call Amanda later with some excuse as to why I couldn't make it.* But just at that moment I walked into the atrium and saw Amanda sitting there. She was laughing with one of the other athletes, and for the first time that day since attending Mass, I felt peaceful.

When Amanda smiled, she radiated the peace of Christ, and I wanted that. I walked in, she smiled, and said, "Hi Maura, I'm so glad you could make it." I sat down next to her thinking, *Just barely.* Once the study began, I was really glad I had chosen to come. All of us athletes knew each other, so there was a sense of familiarity that helped me relax. Amanda started the study with a prayer and then gave us a slight introduction to Varsity Catholic. Since Amanda was an athlete herself, she had been hired by FOCUS to minister to the student-athletes on Seton Hall's campus.

That night we talked about what it was like to be an athlete on campus and explored different ways in which we could spread the Gospel to our teammates. I really enjoyed the time we all spent together that night. I felt comfortable, which was rare for me. It was awesome that several student-athletes could gather around a table and talk about our faith. I was most definitely going back.

As the weeks progressed, I spent more and more time with Amanda. She really challenged me to live out my faith in a radical way, and I welcomed the challenge. Pretty drastic change from the timid athlete who wouldn't even consider going to a Bible study, right? I just needed someone to gently guide me. God knew that I wouldn't respond to the constant, almost aggressive invitations that I had received. He used Amanda's warm and compassionate personality to radically change my life.

At the next Bible study, we talked about humanity's call to greatness. Pope Emeritus Benedict XVI said, "Man was created for greatness-for God Himself; he was created to be filled by

God. But his heart is too small for the greatness to which it is destined. It must be stretched..."[1] We talked about what that really meant and how we could apply it to our lives as student-athletes. Amanda posed the following question to us: "What does it mean to be made for greatness as a student-athlete?" Being a deep thinker, I particularly enjoyed pondering the questions she asked. Amanda made Bible study real for us, and I really liked that.

She encouraged us to look at our lives, and when doing so, it was easy to see that we didn't live comfortable lives as a student-athletes. We had to get up very early for our first practice of the day, and to do that required managing our time wisely so we could go to bed at a decent hour.

"What if you want to be one of the best athletes on your team—what does that take?" she asked. We all knew firsthand the sacrifice and discipline it required. Her questions made studying the Bible relatable.

She asked us if we had ever cut corners during practice. I apprehensively admitted that I had. She pressed further and asked why we cut corners in our respective sports. One of the girls volunteered, "Because they are hard." We all agreed with her. Amanda explained that avoiding discomfort and pain is a natural part of life. Our culture today tries to make everything as easy as possible, so we put forth the least amount of effort, which is why our society is so troubled.

Character stems from virtue, and when we continually seek the easiest way to accomplish a task, we are not striving after virtue. To live a life of greatness demands constant perseverance, and perseverance was something we were all familiar with.

One week at Bible study, Amanda compared Jesus to a sports coach. She asked us, "What type of coach would you have if he always made practice easy? Would you increase your endurance

---

1   Spe Salvi - Encyclical Letter, Benedict XVI." Vatican: the Holy See. Vatican Website. Libreria Editrice Vaticana, 2005. Web. 30 Nov. 2007

level if you never perspired or if your coach never pushed you? Would you have the feeling that you had accomplished something at the end of the workout? Would you be the best athlete you could be?"

Everything Amanda said made sense to me, and I desired to soak up as much of her words as I could. I knew about pushing myself as an athlete. I ran through rain, snow, freezing temperatures, little or no sleep, hunger pains, and other inconveniences. Her questions got me thinking. *Did I give God the same amount of time that I gave to my running? After all, shouldn't I give God more time than running? I mean, He is the one that gave me this athletic talent in the first place. I had two arms, two legs, and a great love for athletics. It was time I started thanking God for the gifts I had in my life.*

People often ask me what initiated a change in my faith journey. I tell them Varsity Catholic is where it all began.

CHAPTER 5
Pornography's Destruction

I n January 2008 I attended the FOCUS conference with my sister Clare and many of our friends in Grapevine, Texas. We sat in a crowded conference room talking and laughing as we awaited the main speaker, Curtis Martin, the founder of FOCUS. You know that tired feeling you get when you attend a conference or retreat? The feeling that comes from traveling to get to the conference, staying up late with friends, and then getting up entirely too early the next day for the day's events? That's how I felt as we waited for Curtis Martin's talk. In all candor, I was hoping his talk would be boring so I could get a quick nap in.

The master of ceremonies walked onstage, and the room suddenly quieted down. Curtis was introduced as thousands of college students applauded. He opened his talk with a statement that changed my life forever. I know that sounds so cliché, but I sincerely mean that with every fiber of my being. "Pornography industries make more money each year than the NFL, MLB, MLS, and NBA."

My heart beat rapidly. I felt like it was going to jump out of my chest. I thought of Charlie, the guy I was dating. *No, he wouldn't look at pornography. He would never go behind my back like that.*

Okay, calm down, Maura, I coached myself. *He is Catholic; you pray the Rosary together. Take a deep breath and try to relax.*

But I couldn't relax. I don't remember another word Curtis said after that, and I felt like I was going to faint. I had fainted before, and it's a horrible feeling. Your vision gets blurry, your hearing slowly diminishes, you become extremely light-headed, your whole body feels numb, and then you just fall over. That's how I felt, except I didn't fall over. I just sat there numb, as soft tears formed in my eyes, gently trickled down my cheeks, and dripped on the pamphlet I was grasping. I remember holding that pamphlet so tightly, as if that would make it all go away somehow.

Clare leaned over to ask if I was okay. I told her I didn't feel well. One of the girls sitting next to me leaned in and whispered, "Yeah, your face is so white, Maura."

"Is it?" I asked as I quietly got up to leave the room. Clare followed me, but I reassured her that I'd be fine and asked her to please sit back down. The last thing I wanted was to make a scene.

I snuck into an empty hallway, sat down on the floor, pulled my legs close to my chest, buried my head in my lap, and wept. The pain was so intense that I just wanted to run away.

After composing myself, I reached into my pocket for my phone and called Charlie. I asked about his day and didn't mention what had just happened. He asked what was wrong, and I told him I was just tired. He said he would call me later to say good night and we said goodbye.

For the next two weeks, I acted as if everything was fine. Inside, however, I was a mess. I didn't say anything to Charlie because I didn't know how. I really liked him and didn't want to lose him. Something inside me, though, just knew he had a struggle with a sexual addiction. It's hard to explain—it's like I had a mother's intuition, but I obviously wasn't his mother . . . or a mother at all yet.

Charlie and I had talked of marriage. He showed me where he wanted us to live and told me the wedding vows he wanted to someday say to me. My heart was a bundle of mixed emotions, and I didn't know what to do.

I went to the Blessed Sacrament and gave my heart to God. I told Him how alone, scared, and broken I felt. It was such a relief to reveal my aching heart. I was afraid to tell anyone else because I feared they wouldn't understand. I begged God to show me some clarity. I knew what I experienced at Curtis Martin's talk was profound.

Why had this happened to me? Was I making this up in my mind? Should I say something to Charlie? Left to my own devices, I didn't know the answers to these questions. So I asked God what to do. I promised Him that I would be still and asked Him to protect me. I was terrified.

I also didn't want to act upon something that wasn't true. *What if everything is really fine, and this is just my imagination?* I was frightened to talk to Charlie because I feared the worst, but I didn't want to entertain those thoughts because of what it would do to my shallow self-esteem.

Two weeks later, without me saying anything, Charlie confessed about his ongoing sexual addiction. At first, I couldn't say anything. I couldn't even cry. Then I turned to fight mode. *We can do this together,* I thought. *I could be his accountability partner. He could go to therapy and talk to a priest. We could fix this.*

A few weeks later we went to a black-tie wedding together. I bought a gorgeous, designer, floor-length black dress. My favorite part of the dress was the tasteful and elegant silver beading in the front, and just beneath the beading was a beautiful piece of black silk that gathered in the center and eloquently flowed down the front of the dress.

I curled my hair, painted my nails, applied red lipstick, and wore strappy black high heels. When I looked in the mirror before leaving my girlfriend's bedroom, all I could see was what I perceived as ugliness. I felt incredibly self-conscious.

I heard Charlie's car pull up to the house, and he came upstairs. "You're gorgeous," he said, beaming. "Come here, I just want to hug you." He pulled me close and held me . . . and I cringed. "You're stunning," he whispered in my ear.

I wanted to forget about his struggle for the night and enjoy my time with him. But self-conscious thoughts flooded through my mind the whole evening. I felt repulsed whenever he kissed me that night, not by him but by his actions. *Why was this so hard for me?*

He smiled at me from across the room as I was talking to a friend. He walked to the bar and ordered a gin and tonic. I just stared at him for a few seconds. I felt so ugly, so betrayed, so hurt. I just wanted to cover up my body with an oversized sweatshirt and run away.

Later that week Charlie told me about his plan to keep his computer in the medical school lab overnight. Initially I thought this was a great idea and encouraged him to keep persevering. Two days later he bought a Blackberry, and that's when I knew I couldn't do it anymore—but I also didn't know how to say goodbye.

Now he has it on his phone, I thought. *It's was right there in his pocket.* That was the night I finally broke down, the first time since the FOCUS conference. I actually experienced relief through my tears that night; I had held them in for so long. I was scared to say goodbye. *What would that look like? What would it feel like?* I was terrified of the unknown. *But surely there must be something more than this,* I thought. I wanted a man to protect and provide for me. Contrary to feeling protected, I felt exceedingly violated. I felt gross.

I went in front of the Blessed Sacrament and asked God what He wanted of me. I knew in my heart that Charlie wasn't the man I was going to marry. My heart ached for a man to mirror God the Father's love toward me, even though at the time I didn't know it. I knew I couldn't be in a relationship with the intention to *fix* a man, but I found it almost impossible to say goodbye. Looking back, I can clearly see that I couldn't be in a healthy relationship with a man until I focused on my own healing and recovery. If I had married Charlie, it would have been a disaster because I didn't have the tools I needed to be in a relationship and deal with all the ups and downs that come with marriage. I am so thankful that God protected me, even though at the time it was so hard for me to understand. One of the most painful parts about the situation was that Charlie ended things with me a few weeks later.

Reflecting on my time with Charlie, I am so grateful that he broke up with me because the pain of losing his friendship cracked my heart open to fill the pain from my father.

"It's not you; it's me," Charlie told me. "You deserve so much more than I can give you." When Charlie said those words, the first thing I thought of was my dad not being there. I thought of the night before my First Holy Communion when he threatened twenty times not to come. I thought of waking up in the middle of the night to see him throwing pictures off the walls with glass shattering everywhere. I thought of all the family vacations he didn't go on and the ones he threatened to take away from us. I thought of our annual summer trip to the water park that he threatened not to take us on. I thought of all the dinners he interrupted with his violence and harsh words. I thought of my artwork that he ripped off the wall and my Irish step dancing trophies he threw out the window in his anger. I thought of all the times when I was a little girl hanging on his legs by the downstairs door, begging him not to leave us.

So many painful memories came to mind when Charlie said those words. This is why the breakup was so hard for me because I had never vocalized the loss of my father. And Charlie's struggle with sexual addiction struck the deepest part of my insecurities and my struggle with body image and self-worth.

CHOOSING TO SEE BEAUTY

CHAPTER 6

Full of Pain

On one particularly chilly winter evening, I was the first to arrive for Bible study, all bundled up in my woolen J.Crew peacoat. I talked to Amanda for a while before the other athletes arrived. I don't remember exactly what we were talking about prior to me mentioning my love for Saint Teresa of Kolkata. But when I mentioned her, Amanda told me about the mission trip to Kolkata, India, that FOCUS sponsored. I jumped out of my chair and said, "Oh my goodness! I've always wanted to go to India! I would love that!" The other girls started arriving, so Amanda said she would email me the application the following morning.

I waited anxiously for Amanda's email the following morning. I knew this was the start of something beautiful—this was going to be the change I so desperately needed. I yearned for something to look forward to besides school, work, and running.

I appeared to have it all together. I spent hours in the library studying, but only my professors knew how poor some of my grades were. I failed a religion class that year because I was too depressed to take the final. I didn't even have the energy to talk about it with my professor. I didn't think he would care or understand, so I accepted the F and had to retake the class. I wondered what was wrong with me.

Why did I have so much trouble getting out of bed in the morning? Why did I only want to wear sweatshirts and sweats? Why did I struggle so much in school? Why did I hate my body? Why did I cry so much? Why did I have nightmares? Why couldn't I just be happy? Why was I always so nervous? Why couldn't I look into people's eyes? I really wanted to be able to look into people's eyes, but despite practicing, I just couldn't seem to do it. When I allowed myself time to think, these were some of the thoughts that ruminated in my mind. But most of the time I told myself I was fine and to keep moving forward. The thought of asking for help was out of the question. I wasn't one of those girls who needed help; I had it together, and I would keep going.

I opened Amanda's email and felt a deep sense of peace. I printed it out so I could read the application questions on the way to class. I couldn't focus in class, but I somehow managed to enter into our class discussion intelligently. I often wondered where my answers came from when called upon by my professors because I had a hard time paying attention most of the time.

After class and evening Mass, I briskly walked back to the library to fill out the India application. My stomach was growling; I was starving. I debated if I should get some dinner before heading to the library. *Well, I don't want to eat dinner now and then lose control when I get home too. I'll just wait until I get home.*

I logged into one of the computers in the library, and that's when the fear of the unknown struck me like a ten-foot wave. Have you ever been swimming in the ocean when a huge wave looks as if it's headed right for you? In an instant you need to decide if you should try and ride the wave to shore or dive deep underneath the surface before it crashes right on you. Well, that's how I felt at that very moment in the library, except my fear was fear of the unknown, fear of rejection, fear of not being enough.

What if they don't accept me? I've never participated in a mission trip before; I've never even been to a soup kitchen. I don't want to get my hopes up for nothing. I wallowed in these thoughts for a few moments and then decided to get serious. *Well, I just have to write a killer application then.* I read over the questions one more time and started writing. After I had answered all of the questions, I decided to pack up my books and drive home.

The next day was Saturday, and after running I always spent a good portion of the day in the library. As soon as I got there Saturday morning, I opened the Word document that I had saved titled *India.* I reread my answers, and after making the necessary grammatical changes, I copied and pasted my answers from the Word document into the application. I glanced over my answers one more time and hit send. *There, that's done—the rest is in God's hands. If He wants me to go, I'll get in; if not, He has something else in store for me this summer.*

In the weeks that followed, I checked my email compulsively awaiting a response from FOCUS. I wasn't sure what to expect, so I tried my best to keep a positive outlook as I waited in the unknown. I reassured myself with optimism, telling myself, If *God wants me to go, I'll get in.*

On a particularly challenging day, ten days after I had submitted my application, I visited the chapel three times during the course of ten hours. The first was for noon Mass; the second before a Biology exam, where I prayed for wisdom and strength to make it to the end of the day. All I really wanted to do was to go home and cry myself to sleep. The pain was so intense that day, and every girl I saw on campus who was dressed inappropriately caused my heart to bleed more. Toward the middle of the day, I just wanted to scream at the highest velocity possible—as if screaming would somehow release the anger within me. Instead I kept it locked in my heart where no one could see it or notice that I was hurting.

I sat in class after my Biology exam, feeling numb. I didn't take notes, participate, or even remotely pay attention for the entire class. I just sat there. When I noticed the other students were closing their laptops and notebooks, I glanced at the clock on the wall. *Yup, it's time to go.*

I glanced down at my blank notebook on my desk, and heard someone say, "Maura, are you all right? You seemed dazed in class; is everything okay?" I looked up to see that it was my professor who had asked those questions.

"Oh, me, I'm fine, just tired," I responded.

"Okay, well, you don't look well. Take care of yourself and I'll see you next time."

It was a crisp night, so I buttoned up my peacoat as I left the Arts and Science building. It was already dark out, and I was relieved because the darkness hid the tears that streamed down my face. *I wasn't fine. And I wasn't just tired. Why do I keep lying to myself and everyone else?* My heart ached, and I walked to the one place that could offer me peace, the chapel. I sat toward the back because I didn't want anyone to see that I had been crying.

I had composed myself at this point and just sat there in the stillness. I tried to form eloquent words to say to God, but I couldn't. Instead, all that came out of my mouth was, "It hurts."

I got up and walked to the back of the chapel and sat on the floor. I pulled my knees up toward my chest and put my forehead on my knees. I wept quietly. Time passed, and then I felt arms wrapped around me. I lifted my head to see Amanda sitting on the floor next to me. Neither of us said anything; we didn't need to. She knew what was troubling me and just held me as I cried. She reached into her bag and handed me a napkin; I wiped my face and softly said, "Thank you." She asked if we could pray together, and we did.

When I left the chapel, she told me to go home and eat dinner. I had a literature test the following day, but knew I was in no disposition to study as planned. *A home-cooked meal and a good night's sleep sound really good*, I thought as I hugged Amanda goodbye, thanked her for her kindness, and walked to my car. I prayed a Rosary on the way home, begging God for the grace of peace, healing, and forgiveness. I prayed for Charlie too. There was a tremendous amount of uncertainty in my life, and I felt as if I was losing control of everything.

My attention span seemed as if it was age-appropriate for a three-year-old child, my grades were dropping, my weight was fluctuating, my binge eating was out of control, my stress fracture didn't feel any better, and I could easily sleep for twenty-plus hours. Charlie was always on my mind. I desperately desired him to be healed of his addiction. I just wanted the pain to disappear.

My mom had made bow-tie pasta with roasted red peppers and grilled chicken for dinner. There were plenty of leftovers, and it felt so good to eat. My stomach had been growling for half the day because all I had eaten was an apple. I was determined not to overeat that night; I had one plate of pasta and promised myself that was it, determined to keep my binging tendencies under control.

After I had eaten, I attempted to review my literature notes for tomorrow's exam. I knew if I went into my room or sat on the couch, I would fall asleep so I stayed at the kitchen table. I felt my phone vibrate in my pocket. *If this is Charlie, I'm not answering.* It was a number I didn't recognize, so I answered it as I walked toward my room.

"Hello, is Maura there?" an unfamiliar voice said.

"This is Maura," I said.

"Hi, Maura, this is Kristen Fausey from FOCUS, the Fellowship of Catholic University Students. I'm calling to invite you to Kolkata, India, this summer with FOCUS."

I was standing facing my dresser, and despite still wearing my peacoat, I got the chills when I heard Kristen's invitation. Hearing her words, I felt God's physical embrace, as if he was telling me, "Maura, you are my daughter, and I love you more than you can fathom. I want you to come to India this summer to get to know Me. I desire for you to experience My love. It hurts Me to see you suffer. Let Me love you through this trip."

As joyful tears formed in my eyes, I told Kristen that I would absolutely love to go. I could hear the excitement in Kristen's voice as she began to explain some of the logistics of the trip to me. I asked who else was going, and she told me that I was the first student she had called.

She told me she would send me some information about applying for a visa in India, the vaccines I would need, and how to fundraise. As I said goodbye to Kristen, I felt tremendous peace within. Despite all of the uncertainty in my life, one thing was constant: God loved me and would never stop pursuing me. Kristen's phone call filled my heart with hope.

The next day I walked into the chapel with a renewed sense of God's love for me. I knelt and thanked Him for Kristen's phone call and for this opportunity to travel to India and serve the poor. I told Him how excited I was and asked Him to please help me fundraise all of the money I needed.

Two days later, Lucy, the other female missionary from FOCUS that was going to India, called me to introduce herself and to say that she was going to help me fundraise for the trip. The trip cost three thousand dollars. Could I ever raise even close to that amount? During those times God whispered to me through my anxiety, "Maura, you are my daughter; I will provide for you. Trust Me."

CHAPTER 7

Meeting Mary in India

I thought I was *tough* because I was a competitive long-distance runner and soccer player. I thought I would surely be able to handle India.

Wow! God must have been laughing at my ignorance, I thought as we rode from the airport to our living accommodations that first afternoon in Kolkata. The poverty, illnesses, smells, heat, noise, and crowds were tremendous.

During that first ride from the airport, I saw families living under tents made of garbage bags. Others were just living on the curbside, without any protection from inclement weather. Their children were naked and sleeping in filth. Neither adults nor children knew where their next morsel of food would come from. I sat there in the taxi, mystified. *Dear Jesus, thank you for my life. Thank you for this opportunity to serve these people, please give me the grace to serve them heroically. Please help me to get to know you better, for I truly desire that.*

In India, people take taxis, buses, or walk to commute. Since we were staying at a small convent, forty-five minutes from the airport, our group squeezed into two taxis. Taxis in India are half the size of the taxis in the United States, and half the time the drivers don't know where they are going, all of which coincided with the sense of adventure of our mission. When we finally arrived at our destination, we took a moment to pray as a group.

The convent we stayed at wasn't related to the Missionaries of Charity. Due to the large quantity of volunteers that travel to India each year, no volunteers are permitted to stay with the Missionaries of Charity. Where we stayed was one of the cleanest places I entered in India, which was a tremendous blessing. There was running water, toilets, and a bed with a five-inch mattress for each of us.

It was a fifteen-minute walk to the Mother House, which is where Saint Teresa lived and died, and where many of her sisters live today. Saint Teresa's tomb is also on the main level of the house, which makes it accessible for visitors and volunteers to come in and pray there. We didn't need time to unpack when we arrived, since we only brought the bare necessities, so we walked to the Mother House to pray a holy hour by Mother Teresa's tomb. We all struggled to stay awake since we were adjusting to a thirteen-hour time difference. It was the middle of the night our time, which was the afternoon in India.

Walking through the streets for the first time in India was an experience I will never forget. People went to the bathroom, bathed, slaughtered animals, and threw their trash right on the street. The filth and stench were overwhelming and could easily cause a person to pass out. The poor would hang on us, begging for food and money because we were American, and they perceived us to be rich. This was heart-wrenching because if you gave to one person, a dozen more would quickly flock to your side. And we simply didn't have money or food to give to everyone.

When we reached the Mother House for the first time that afternoon, I was almost relieved. I felt a sense of safety within the containment of the Mother House walls. Desperately needing a moment to myself, I knelt before Mother Teresa's tomb to thank God once again for this experience. When I arose from kneeling, I went to sit against the wall in the back of the room to pray. Mother Teresa's tomb was in the center of a fairly large room with a few scattered benches. I chose to sit on the floor because God has almost always met me in my darkest moments on the floor, and I feel closer to Him when sitting there. I sat in silence and contemplated all that had just happened within the past twenty-four hours.

Being still before God for an hour was new to me, as I had never prayed in silence for more than fifteen minutes before. The Lord knew I needed a strong dose of humility, and that's just what I got. I struggled to remain still and dozed off several times due to extreme exhaustion. *I wonder if anyone else is this tired? Wow, these holy hours are hardcore! I'm not sure if I'm going to be able to sit still for this long every day. No wonder FOCUS missionaries are so holy!*

I glanced around the room and saw several bobbing heads, as many from our group struggled to stay awake. *I should seriously be focusing on praying,* I thought to myself. *God, please help me to focus and grant me the grace to stay awake.* Just then I heard a thud, so I looked up to see Joel. He had been sitting on one of the benches and had fallen asleep and then had fallen off the bench. I chuckled, thinking, *Well, it must be okay that I'm falling asleep because Joel fell asleep, and he's a missionary.*

I thought I had to appear perfect before God in prayer, but that summer I learned how false my thought process was. God takes us just as we are. When we come before Him, He is enthralled by us—not by our sinfulness, but by the beauty we possess being created in His image and likeness. That summer I learned countless lessons, the greatest of which was the message of God as my Father. The profound love that I experienced that summer from God the Father would change the rest of my existence.

Our days in India were long. We arose at 5:00 a.m., and thirty minutes later, we gathered outside the convent to pray as a group before walking to the Mother House for 6:00 a.m.

Mass. Our theme for the mission trip was Hebrew 12:1–2, which Kristen had printed on index cards for each of us:

Therefore, since we are surrounded by so great a cloud of witnesses, let us also lay aside every weight, and sin which clings so closely, and let us run with endurance the race that is set before us, looking to Jesus, the founder and perfecter of our faith, who for the joy that was set before him endured the cross, despising the shame, and is seated at the right hand of the throne of God.

With that verse in our hearts, we made the Sign of the Cross, lathered our legs and arms with bug repellent, and began our journey to the Mother House. Each morning on our walk we were greeted by many of the same faces from the street, since the street was their home. I often felt as if we were intruding on their space. Some would still be sleeping on blankets or garbage bags. I often wondered how they could sleep with the amount of noise from the honking horns of buses and taxis. As the days passed, various children grew accustomed to our presence and often waited for us each morning with their soccer balls, hoping we would play with them.

Arriving at the Mother House each morning was one of the highlights of my day. The warmth, joy, and gentleness that the sisters possessed was comforting. As we walked up the two flights of stairs that separated us from the chapel, we could hear the angelic voices of the sisters. The first time I heard their exquisite voices, I was convinced this must be a glimpse of Heaven. After Mass, all of the volunteers who served with the Missionaries of Charity gathered downstairs for a breakfast provided by the sisters.

Toward the back of the room, there was a long table with four plastic containers filled with slices of bread and bananas. Bananas in India could be up to a third of the size of bananas in the United States. There was also chai tea to drink, which is a very common drink in India. I missed my dark roasted coffee very much.

Breakfast was a great opportunity to meet people from a vast range of cultures and countries, and it was interesting to hear everyone's story about why they wanted to travel to India to serve with the Missionaries of Charity, or how long they had been in India serving. When everyone had eaten, we all gathered to pray before journeying to our various work sites. Our voices joined together in one accord to recite the following prayer by John Henry Newman:

Dear Jesus, help me to spread Your fragrance everywhere I go.
Flood my soul with Your spirit and life.
Penetrate and possess my whole being so utterly,
That my life may only be a radiance of Yours.
Shine through me, and be so in me
That every soul I come in contact with
May feel Your presence in my soul.
Let them look up and see no longer me, but only Jesus!
Stay with me and then I shall begin to shine as You shine,
So to shine as to be a light to others;
The light, O Jesus will be all from You; none of it will be mine;
It will be you, shining on others through me.
Let me thus praise You the way You love best,
by shining on those around me.
Let me preach You without preaching,
not by words but by my example,
By the catching force of the sympathetic influence of what I do,
The evident fullness of the love my
heart bears to You. Amen.

After a unified Amen, we all dispersed to various homes throughout the city. In the mornings, Kristen, Eric, Lucy, Tyler, and I served at Kalighat, which is Mother Teresa's Home for the

Dying. Kalighat was roughly thirty minutes from the Mother House, so we took a twenty minute bus ride and walked the remainder of the way.

The first time I stepped off the bus onto the filthy streets of the city to walk the rest of the way to Kalighat, I was submerged in thought. *What is this home going to be like? What if I don't know what to do? What if I don't feel useful? What if I don't know how to love them?*

For months I had been preparing for this moment, and now that it had arrived, I didn't know what to do with these emotions. I turned to God. *Jesus, please help me to love these patients. Please give me the grace to embrace these next weeks with love and total service to You, through the poor. Saint Teresa, please pray for me.* The noise in the streets that morning was particularly vexing, so I tried to block it out and mentally prepare for Kalighat as the five of us walked together in silence.

When I entered Kalighat for the first time, I just stood there, paralyzed. After several moments of silence, I pondered several thoughts, with the most prominent being, *This is where these patients are going to die. God, please help me love them as You would. Please help me with Your grace.*

Kalighat is divided into two sections—one for male patients and the other for female patients, with each volunteer serving on their gender-appropriate sides. There is a room in between the two sections where Mass is celebrated and another room on the lower level where the patients' clothes and dishes are washed. The second level of the home is the rooftop, which is where all of the volunteers gathered mid-morning for a break and where we also hung the patients' wet clothes to dry.

One of the most exceedingly profound experiences happened that summer at Kalighat. The sisters cautioned us about becoming too close to an individual patient because *every* patient needed care. They also were also aware of the emotional bond the volunteers develop with the patients and the reality that their life expectancy wasn't long. There was one patient who particularly captured my heart and showed me the love of the Father.

"Excuse me, can you come help me?" said one of the sisters. I walked over to her and asked how I could help. "Please help me with this patient. I need to remove her bandage."

"Of course, of course," I said, as I sat on the bed next to this dying woman. The nurse told me she would be right back and asked me to stay with her. As she walked away, I thought, *Here is an opportunity to love. How do I show this dying woman the love of Christ?* She was lying there in a fetal position, probably weighing only seventy pounds. Her eyes were tightly closed, as if her contracted eyelids were elevating some of the immense pain she was experiencing. I wasn't sure what to do.

I thought of Amanda and the time she came over to me when I was sitting on the chapel floor. Amanda sat on the floor next to me and held me in a tight embrace as I cried. Instantaneously I knew what to do. I slowly moved closer to the dying woman so as not to frighten her and tenderly lifted her beautiful, emaciated body into my arms. I took her wrinkled hand in mine as her eyes remained tightly closed. The nurse returned just as the woman turned her head abruptly to one side. As she did this, the lightly wrapped bandage around her head fell off, revealing her skull. Besides studying biology, I had never seen anything that more closely resembled the human brain than what was before me, for this didn't just *resemble* the human brain. This *was* the human brain, and it was mere inches away from me.

Obviously, this woman had no hair on her head, along with the skin that normally covers a person's skull. Looking at her head, one could see the various lobes of the brain—it was completely exposed. The nurse told me that we needed to finish removing whatever skin remained with a pair of scissors, and as we did this, I could see tiny heads protruding from her brain.

"What are those?" I asked, pointing to the dots that were trying to wiggle their way from beneath her brain.

"Those are worms, and we need to get them out. She is dying of brain cancer. Do you think you can stomach it?" Sister asked.

I thought my heart was going to pound right out of my chest, but I answered, "Yes, of course. What are we going to take the worms out with?"

"With this," the nurse said, as she handed me a pair of tweezers. We pulled out as many worms as we could in our patient's brain, and then we moved to her legs, which contained over a hundred.

She continued to keep her eyes closed, even though she was awake. And though she never spoke and there was an obvious language barrier, I wanted to talk to her. I asked the nurse if she knew her name, and she told me no one knew. Knowing that she wouldn't be able to understand me, I named her Mary. I gently whispered to her, and she squeezed my hand with astounding force for her stature. We had no pain medication to give her, so I knew the strength of her grasp on my hand only portrayed a portion of the pain she was enduring. When we were finished, we bandaged her head with a clean dressing, and I remained by her side and softly rubbed her back as she slept.

As the days at Kalighat turned to weeks, it grew even more emotionally draining. We would be washing dishes with our hands or the patients' clothes with our hands and feet and see dead bodies being brought in and out. I would often wake up several times throughout the night due to the immense heat and stench, and during this time I prayed for the patients at Kalighat that I loved deeply. The reality that a certain patient may not be there the following morning caused my sensitive heart to worry. I wanted to help them all and struggled with the unrealistic aspect of such a quest.

One of the greatest things I feared was saying goodbye to the patients at Kalighat, so I yearned to savor every moment as the inevitable day drew near. On our last day to serve at Kalighat, I woke up at 3:00 a.m. I anxiously feared that Mary and a few of the other patients that I had bonded with would be dead. Tears streamed down my face as I lay there in bed. I clenched my Rosary beads and prayed.

When we arrived at Kalighat several hours later, I scurried to Mary's bedside to find her still breathing. Her eyes remained closed as she lay there in her usually fetal position, riddled in pain. *Oh, thank you, Jesus, that she is still alive! Thank you so much! I don't know what I would have done if I couldn't have said goodbye to her. Thank you for bringing Mary into my life. I really see You in her. Please help me to love her as You would today!*

No one had died that night, and there were a few new faces on the woman's side that humid summer morning. I went about my usual tasks of helping feed the patients breakfast and washing and hanging clothes on the roof, all while keeping Mary close to my heart. When I had finished, I went to her side, clasped her hand in mine, and knelt down so our faces were close. Her eyes remained closed as I prayed. I glanced at my watch. *I only have one more hour here. Only one more hour to be with Mary.* My heart was heavy; I loved her deeply and saying goodbye seemed impossible. *God, please give me the grace when the time comes.*

I walked over to one of the cabinets that held what limited medical supplies Kalighat had and reached for one of the bottles of hand lotion. Mary's skin was shriveled and dry due to the immense heat and lack of nutrients. I lathered her whole body with the cream five times as she continued to sleep. The first few times that I gently massaged her with the cream, it immediately soaked into her skin. I kept applying the cream until her skin seemed soft, which I hoped would make her feel more comfortable. I wanted her to feel loved and die with dignity. I gazed down at my watch again: ten minutes left. I longed for time to pause so I could stay with Mary a little longer.

I put the cream back in the cabinet and walked to Mary's bedside for the last time. I tenderly placed both my hands on her head and prayed over her as she slept. My last prayer for her was that if God willed it, He would relieve her of all pain so she could die in peace—and that He would let me carry it for her. I prayed, "Jesus, if You so desire, please give me her pain. And if this would please You, may she open her eyes, look straight at me for the first time, and smile. May Mary please die in peace, Jesus, free from pain."

Mary continued to sleep as I traced a sign of the cross on her forehead. I lingered for a moment and then walked away. I walked five steps and turned to take what I promised God would be *one final glance.* To my complete astonishment, she had opened her eyes, and I raced back to her side. I sat on the floor with my elbows on her bed so I could see her eyes. She reached for my hand and tenderly squeezed it, and for the first time, it wasn't a squeeze of pain. One tear fell from her right eye as she looked directly at me and smiled! It was the most beautiful smile I had ever seen in my life!

Tears formed in my eyes and gently rolled down my cheeks and onto her mattress. As I lovingly placed my hand on top of hers, my body suddenly grew cold. I glanced at my arm, which was covered in tiny goosebumps—in the 118 degree heat. Jesus was right there! Mary will forever hold a special place inside my heart, and the world's most renowned writer could never compose a string of words deep enough to adequately describe my encounter with her.

CHAPTER 8

Learning to Pray in India

Toward the middle of our mission, we took an overnight train ride to visit Darjeeling, located in the hill country of the Himalayas. We were able to rest during the night on thin cots that hung from the wall. They looked like bunk beds, with top and bottom cots.

During the night several men roamed the train in search of money and valuable possessions and since we were American, they assumed we would possess both items, although we had none. A strange man touching me during the night petrified me, so I tried to stay awake, sleeping only ten minutes at a time. It was a long night.

I watched the sun rise through one of the windows on the train, and its beautiful shades of yellow and orange greatly relieved my fear. *Ah, morning, I am so glad to welcome a new day and see the sunrise and put last night behind me.* I prayed morning prayer with Eric and Tyler as my stomach growled. I was starving, as we all were, and ate handfuls of granola for breakfast. When we arrived in Darjeeling, we had a three-hour jeep ride up the Himalayas, which was breathtaking!

On the train to Darjeeling is where Mother Teresa first received the call from God to start the Missionaries of Charity. Darjeeling was gorgeous and a much-needed reprieve from the boisterous and destitution of the city. I enjoyed praying a holy hour without the sound of the honking taxis that populated

Kolkata. Our team used Darjeeling as a time to regain our strength for the remainder of our mission. We were able to do some sightseeing, shopping, tea drinking, reflective prayer, and hiking. I bought several silk scarfs, some as gifts and two for myself. I loved their vibrant colors and soft texture.

One of my favorite adventures was rising at 3:00 a.m. with Nathan and Stephanie to hike to the top of one of the mountains. Since Darjeeling is nestled in the hill country, the air was much cooler than Kolkata, which we all appreciated. It felt so good to put on a sweatshirt. That morning the air was refreshing and invigorating and was actually cool enough for a woolen hat, which Nathan generously let me borrow many times that trip. Hiking to the top of the mountain was amazing. We reached the summit just as the sun was rising, and the view was spectacular. Without announcing it, the three of us stood there in silence for a few minutes to relish the splendor arrayed before us. *I wonder how anyone could view this scenery and not believe in You, God. You're amazing! Thank you for displaying your glory and majesty to us through Your creation.*

Before traveling home to the United States, we spent three days in Goa, located in South West India. Upon arriving, we were all incredibly excited because Goa is more Western than Kolkata, so there were toilets and showers. We all used the restroom at the airport, and you would have thought we had never seen a toilet before. The simple things in life that we took for granted in the United States started to excite us all. I particularly enjoyed taking a hot shower and sleeping on a mattress thicker than a few inches. Both experiences were glorious! In Goa we were able to visit and pray at the tomb of Saint Francis Xavier, one of the patron saints of missionaries. We were also able to go to the Indian Ocean, which made me miss home.

When we got back to Kolkata, we were able to attend the final profession of vows for the Missionaries of Charity, which is the final yes after nine-and-a-half years of discernment. Several of us were also able to clean the church where this ceremony took place. We spent a long morning dusting, mopping, and scrubbing on our hands and knees. What struck me was that the sisters who cleaned with us never took a break, but they insisted that we stop and rest mid-morning. Their strength proved remarkable, and they were always smiling too.

Before leaving Kolkata for Goa, we were able to meet with Sister Nirmala, who at the time was Saint Teresa's successor. She gave each of us a relic and a medal of Saint Teresa.

Being in her presence was an experience I'll never forget, as we were able to talk and laugh with a living saint! And one day I had the honor of scanning hundreds of pictures of Mother Teresa into the Missionaries of Charity's computer; these were being used for her canonization.

After Kalighat, in the afternoons I served at Shishu Bhavan, which is an orphanage for abandoned and mentally and physically handicapped children. Most of the children who lived there were severely handicapped. Many were blind and autistic, but all were exceedingly loved by the sisters and volunteers. Most of my time involved playing with the children and doing various physical therapy exercises with them. Feeding the children dinner always presented a challenge, as most of the children could not sit without assistance and would fling their heads in various directions. They would also use their hands to knock over their dinner if it was within their reach. Sometimes the sisters had to tie them to their seats just so we could feed them all. We finished our evening shifts by 5:30 p.m. After that we all met at the Mother House to pray a holy hour with the sisters in front of the Blessed Sacrament.

Even though by the end of the day I was physically and emotionally exhausted, I eagerly awaited to spend time with Jesus in front of the Blessed Sacrament. In the beginning it was hard for me to sit still for an hour. The heat gave us no reprieve in the evening, and while kneeling, pools of sweat would puddle under and around our knees. The noise of the taxis made it difficult to focus, and the pungent aroma of the city greatly upset my stomach, often bringing me to the verge of passing out. I was starving, but everything I ate passed right through me. I often thought about all of the times I had complained about my mom's cooking. My mom is an amazing cook, but I still managed to complain. When I emailed her from India, I told her I would do anything for a bowl of her lentil soup, which is something I always managed to grumble about. I would daydream about a big bowl of it, with the steam still rising from the bowl. My mom always served it with grated Swiss cheese and thick slices of cornbread. I put raspberry jam on my cornbread at home, and I could almost taste its sweetness in my mouth whenever I thought about it.

When I wasn't daydreaming about food during our holy hours, I tried to pray. God truly worked on my heart each day in India, especially during our holy hours. I tried to give Him all of the uncomfortable aspects of the mission so He could make good out of them. I told Him I desperately longed to unite my sufferings to His on the cross. I asked Him for grace and guidance about how to love the patients at Kalighat and the children at Shishu Bhavan. I learned to sit in His presence and be still before the Creator of the universe. During one holy hour in India, I examined my prayer life prior to India, in which I mainly prayed the Rosary and Chaplet of Divine Mercy and read. These are perfectly acceptable forms of prayer, but I needed to learn how to listen to God and be still in His presence, which is exceedingly vital.

About halfway through the mission, Eric gave a talk on prayer which really helped put things in perspective for me. God also used Eric that afternoon to teach me about Himself and who He is as Father.

I didn't know how to start a holy hour, and I felt embarrassed to ask anyone how they started their prayer time. I mean, people had told me to talk to God like a friend, but you don't start a holy hour by saying, "Hi, God," do you? How are you supposed to address the King of the universe?

Eric spoke to us about the acronym ACTS, something I had never heard of before. He explained the acronym and said that when we pray, we should incorporate it into our prayer, and this helped me tremendously. The A stands for *adoration*, which means putting yourself in the presence of God and having a wonder for His glory. "Your love, O Lord, extends to the heavens, your faithfulness to the clouds" (Psalm 36:5).

The C is for *contrition*. During this time, one should possess sorrow for one's sins and ask for forgiveness and the grace to amend one's sinful ways. "If we confess our sins, he is faithful and just, and will forgive us our sins and cleanse us from all unrighteousness" (1 John 1:9).

The T of the acronym signifies *thanksgiving*. During this time we should reflect on all the blessings God has bestowed upon us. "Let them give thanks to the Lord for his steadfast love, for his wonderful works to the sons of men" (Psalm 107:15).

S stands for *supplication*, which means asking God, like a child, for the things that you desire, if they are His will. "Ask, and it will be given you; seek, and you will find; knock, and it will be opened for you. For everyone who asks receives, and he who seeks finds, and to him who knocks it will be opened" (Matthew 7:7–8).

I truly am blessed to have many defining moments in my life, moments that have built upon each other in my healing journey. The next portion of Eric's talk was just such a moment. Eric began to shift his focus on how to pray to talk about God as Father. It was a title of God that I didn't know but yearned to. It was a title I feared, yet I was intrigued about all at the same time.

As a young child, teenager, and college student, I often heard my Uncle Paul refer to God as our Father in Heaven during grace before meals over the holidays or family gatherings. Every time I heard him speak of God this way, I wondered what he meant. I wanted to ask him, but I feared my question would be perceived as stupid.

So I grew up wondering who this mysterious Father was and often pondered over Uncle Paul's words. *I wonder if I can talk to God like Uncle Paul does? He talks to Him as if he knows Him. When and where did he encounter Him? When will I know Him?* For years I reflected on these questions, but it wasn't until I got involved with Varsity Catholic and went to India that my heart finally rested in the Truth.

As Eric spoke about God, my heart screamed silently, *This is it! This is what I have been searching for; this is the answer. This is the Truth.* I couldn't fathom someone loving me the way Eric described God loving us. He used adjectives to describe God the Father that were foreign to me. He said God was gentle, loving, merciful, understanding, compassionate, and that He adored us. It was exceedingly challenging for me to digest what Eric was saying. But there was something about God the Father that captivated me. Even though I didn't know Him or understand how He could love me, I desperately craved love—and not the counterfeit love that the world offers, but genuine authentic love, the love of the Father.

After Eric's talk, I went up to him in tears. "Eric, I want to know God the way you know him. Can you teach me?" I asked. Eric knew nothing of my story and offered me the most practical advice, advice I still treasure to this day. One of the things he told me was that in order to know God, I must frequent the sacraments. So I recommitted to going to daily Mass, confession and prayer before the Blessed Sacrament.

God was my Father, too, and I could talk to Him anytime I desired. The way Eric described God mystified me. I glanced toward the crucifix and smiled, because at last I was beginning to understand who this Father was. He was mine. Tears formed in my eyes, softy dripping down my cheeks and onto the pages of my notebook. I was loved. And this love of the Father moved me to tears. My eyes turned from the crucifix to my notebook. I had written many of Eric's words in my journal, but the moisture from my tears had smudged them. Some of my tears had formed droplets on my paper and the ink had diffused into particles of black specks. Whatever I lost on paper, though, adhered to my heart. After Eric's talk, I went to the chapel upstairs by myself to pray.

Choosing to See Beauty

CHAPTER 9

Suicidal Thoughts

After my mission trip to India, I prayed a daily holy hour in front of the Blessed Sacrament. I found this to be essential, and I truly believe that I am alive today because of the graces from those times in Jesus' presence. I experienced tremendous highs and lows after India and was still deeply struggling. I had never told anyone about the abuse or my struggle with body image and food.

One night my mom told me that Charlie's addiction was my fault and that I couldn't even "keep a man." Her words penetrated my heart deeply. I desperately wanted Charlie to love me, and even though he had broken up with me, I was definitely not over him.

That night I got in my car and just started driving. Ten minutes into my drive, I just started screaming as the tears rushed down my face. "Who am I? Why am I here? Does my life even matter? What's my purpose? Why does no one love me? Why does everyone always leave me? What's wrong with me? Are you my Father or not?"

I heard nothing, and the silence made me cry even more. The pain made me feel numb, and I just wanted to feel something, so I accelerated. Driving at an exceedingly dangerous speed, I screamed out again, "Who am I?" Again, I heard nothing so I accelerated to an even more dangerous speed, as my tears started to cloud my vision, which only accentuated the danger of my driving.

You're worthless. You will never be enough. Nobody cares about you, and you'll never be good enough for a man to want you. Your body is ugly and will never be beautiful. See, Charlie had to look at naked pictures of other women because you aren't good enough. You'll never amount to anything, and the pain will never end, so just end the pain now. End it here and now and free yourself of this misery. Slam your car into the median and you will be free of the pain. Do it now.

The urge to take my life was so strong that I accelerated for a third time. I switched lanes to be closer to the median. I kept hearing, *End the pain.* I desperately wanted the pain to end, but I knew in my heart that this would mean the devil had won. And if I lived, the one and only reason would be that the devil wouldn't win this battle. I was worth more than that. So I shouted for a third time, "Who am I? Do you love me?"

The Rosary beads that I brought to India and touched to Mother Teresa's tomb were wrapped around my rearview mirror, and they started to sway vigorously. I remember thinking it odd that they didn't sway before that moment because I was going over one hundred miles an hour. In that moment I heard in my heart, *Maura, you are my daughter. You are precious in my sight, and you are more beautiful than you can imagine. I am your Father, and I love you.*

The Rosary beads immediately stopped swaying, and I switched lines as I slowed down. In my heart I felt a peace I can't even describe. I pulled my car over and just sat there, grateful to be alive. I knew God had saved my life that night.

I don't know what I would have done that night on the highway if I didn't have God. I am confident when I say that I know why people commit suicide. There is nothing to live for, the pain consumes you, and you feel as if there is no way out. But with God, there is hope—hope for a healing, hope for forgiveness, hope for a change, and hope to live for more than what our secular world offers. I clung to this hope.

In front of the Blessed Sacrament each day, I learned how to be still before our Creator. I cried and laughed with Him. I told Him my fears, how much it hurt, how angry I was, how I couldn't look at my reflection anymore, how afraid I was, how worried I was about Charlie, and how lonely I felt. I also thanked Him for this cross He asked me to carry. I told Him I could only do it with His grace, and I begged for the grace to love this cross. I also asked Him to lovingly place the cross on my shoulders each morning and give me the grace to carry it with love.

I want to introduce you to the man who taught me about the power, beauty, and freedom of forgiveness. His name is Dr. Joe Burns. Dr. Burns is a former professor at the Augustine Institute in Denver, Colorado. He graduated from Colorado State University in 1973 and spent twenty years as an Air Force officer and flight instructor in both B-52 and B-1 bombers. He is a distinguished graduate of Squadron Officer School and Combat Crew Training School. He holds master's degrees in both Theological Studies and Management. Dr. Burns is a devout Catholic and has dedicated his life to serving Christ's Church.

It was May 22, 2009, and I was in Colorado taking a week of graduate classes at the Augustine Institute. That morning I got up before dawn to go for a run in the mountains with another student. We returned in time to shower and make it to Mass on time. The chapel was a fourth of a mile walk from where we were staying, and as I was walking that morning, Dr. Burns was headed that way too. He was walking about thirty feet ahead of me by himself. I recognized him from a picture I had seen, but I had never formally met him. I suddenly darted ahead so I could meet him, not even sure why.

As I approached him, I extended my hand and introduced myself. "Hi, I'm Maura. It's a pleasure to meet you." I immediately sensed his distinct presence. He radiated peace yet kept close to himself. He intrigued me.

Once inside the chapel, he sat in the last row by himself. I sat several rows in front of him, and when I turned around to exchange the Sign of Peace with the woman behind me, I saw him again. I knew in my heart that I was in the presence of a devout man. *I wonder what his story is and what he is going to talk about this morning.*

Dr. Burns was our third professor and speaker that morning, and I sat up a little straighter when he walked in. The week proved to be exceedingly condensed, and I was exhausted. I dosed during the lecture prior to Dr. Burn's arrival and was determined to vigorously take notes during his class.

He began by speaking about the New Evangelization and how the Church exists to evangelize. Being completely candid, I was slightly disappointed because I had heard countless talks on the New Evangelization, and it was a little boring. *Really? Is this what he is going to talk about? Why did I think his talk was going to be different?* I sat there listening and drinking watered-down coffee. *I could really use a real cup of coffee or a few shots of espresso,* I thought. Then Dr. Burns said, "Is forgiveness possible?" *What? You were just talking about the New Evangelization, and I was daydreaming about a good cup of coffee. How did we jump from that to forgiveness?*

I instantaneously snapped to attention. Dr. Burns proceeded to share a true story about someone who abused him as a child. The entire class was still. There was one particular day from his childhood that he described that caused me to quiver. I saw my dad in his story, and I started to relive a memory I had repressed for years. Tears began to well in my eyes, and then Dr. Burns paused and glanced at me, as if to say, "I hear you. I see you. I know that pain." He continued his story, and my gentle tears turned to weeping. I was so embarrassed, but I literally couldn't control myself. Dr. Burns paused again and said he was available after class to speak with me. I nodded, as he continued his story. I excused myself to step outside the classroom.

When I returned, he paused a third time. The whole class could see his pain, and this time he cried. *A grown man is crying in front of all of us,* I thought with amazement. The fact that Dr. Burns needed to compose himself was comforting to me; it made me feel like it was okay to cry. I always thought that crying portrayed a sign of weakness. But Dr. Burns' vulnerability appeared courageous. He wasn't weak; he was brave. *If it's okay for him to cry, then surely it's fine for me too.*

When he had finished describing the trauma, the class sat aghast. Then he articulated to us how he encountered reconciliation. He was driving through Texas and listening to a tape by Ann Murchison. She started talking about forgiveness. Her message expressed simplicity to the average listener, yet to the one harmed by the hand of another, it proved daunting. She said that when we forgive from deep within, we not only free ourselves but the abuser as well. God's grace and our free will to choose to forgive will release the one who has caused harm. Dr. Burns said we must forgive in order to be forgiven, and this requires grace. To master this task, as much as any sinner can, he told us to frequent the sacraments. "God promises that He will not give us anything we can't handle," he said. "You have to ask God in prayer to show you how to forgive."

What? Show me how to forgive? That's so hard, and it hurts too. Shouldn't my dad be sorrowful? Why can't he come to me? He was in the wrong, not me. I was just a child. I arose from my seat to go to the restroom to wash my face. As I walked to the restroom, I was tempted to just go back to my room, curl up in bed, and cry. My heart ached, but I desired to be strong, despite this adversity. *How do I do that? You go straight to the restroom, wash your face, get some water, and go back to the classroom to hear the end of Dr. Burns' talk,* I told myself. And that's what I did.

Dr. Burns concluded his talk by telling us that after he heard Ann's lecture, he pulled over to the side of the ride and begged God to help him live out His message of forgiveness, to truly forgive from the heart. As Dr. Burns grew in wisdom over the years, he said that he also learned he needed to forgive himself for believing that the abuse was his fault.

Dr. Burns spoke at length with me after his talk. He was kind, empathetic, and compassionate. He was the first person with whom I shared about the abuse I had experienced. It felt good to talk about it to someone who understood, and it felt comforting to be heard. He greatly encouraged, challenged, and humbled me by his witness. He hugged me goodbye, promised to stay in touch, and reassured me that I could always reach out to him.

Before flying home to New Jersey, I knelt in front of the Blessed Sacrament and thanked God for Dr. Burns and for the opportunity to grow in virtue. *Father, thank you for this week in Colorado and for this opportunity to be challenged. I really want to live out Dr. Burns' talk. I want to be able to forgive—the hurt and pain are too much to hold on to. I desire to let it go. But I need Your help, Your grace, and Your strength. With You, forgiveness is possible; teach me how to forgive and show others Your fatherly love.*

I remained in Jesus' presence for the remainder of the hour. I loved the peace the Blessed Sacrament radiated—everything seemed easier there. The challenge would be in living out what I learned. I knew it would be difficult, but the freedom produced is liberating, Dr. Burns had said, and my heart yearned for that emancipation. Forgiveness is a choice, and I am exceedingly blessed to have met Dr. Burns. He is one of the most humble, courageous, and encouraging people I have ever met.

CHAPTER 10

Cracking Open

*A*fter college I joined the FOCUS staff with Varsity Catholic. I had a great zeal to help other student-athletes discover their worth and dignity as Amanda had helped me. There is a tremendous amount of pressure being a student-athlete, and I loved the mission of Varsity Catholic. Being a missionary with FOCUS painfully revealed how unwell I truly was, however. I needed to first take care of myself before I could give to others through ministry. This was really hard for me to understand, and I felt like I was being *punished* for having an abusive father.

FOCUS generously sent me to IPS (Institute for the Psychological Sciences, part of Divine Mercy University), which was the catalyst for my healing. I went there for a grueling two days of testing. Clare was so kind and drove me there. We stayed for a few days at the hotel across the street and made many memories together when I wasn't at the clinic. I was so embarrassed that I needed a psychological evaluation. The professionals at IPS helped me to see that I had experienced tremendous trauma, that it was okay to talk about it and to get help. The following notes explain the evaluation I underwent and what they advised for me moving forward.

Maura is a twenty-four-year-old single Caucasian female who presented to the IPS Psychology Clinic for a psychological evaluation on March 12–13, 2010. She presented in casual dress and appeared calm and friendly in demeanor on both days. She participated in a lengthy (approximately three hours) clinical interview, and completed five psychological tests, including the Minnesota Multiphasic Personality Inventory, 3rd ed. (MCMI-III), the Thematic Apperception Test (TAT), the Rorschach Inkblot Test, and projective drawings.

On March 12, 2010, Maura reviewed and signed the Informed Consent Form and completed the MMPI-2 and MCMI-III. She behaved in a cooperative and compliant demeanor during this process, although she displayed a tendency to dart her eyes away from the examiner frequently, possibly indicating some felt anxiety. She indicated that she understood the directions, took a reasonable amount of time to complete the tests (about one-and-a-half hours for the MMPI-2 and a half hour for the MCMI-III) and took no breaks while completing them.

On March 13, 2010, Maura completed the Rorschach Inkblot Test, the Thematic Apperception Test, projective drawing, and the clinical interview. During the clinical interview, she was again noticed darting her eyes away from the examiner while conversing and was asked about it. She at first claimed not to notice that she does this, but upon further probing, acknowledged that she does this "because of the abuse." She explained that she has difficulty looking people in the eye because of trust issues, and she attributes this to the past violence and abuse. Other than this apparent anxiety, Maura appeared compliant and put forth a reasonable effort to answer questions in a forthright manner.

When taking the Rorschach Inkblot Test, she seemed more anxious and displayed some resistance by rejecting a card and then started to cry. When informed that the test protocol is invalid because she rejected the card and did not provide a sufficient number of responses, Maura became upset. She requested that the test be readministered, *so that she could have another chance. The test was readministered on the same day, and although Maura provided a sufficient number of responses, the test was judged to be invalid.*

PERSONALITY FUNCTIONING
Validity:

Maura approached the testing process in an open and honest manner and appeared to exert a reasonable effort on each test. The validity indices on the MMPI-2 and the MCMCI-III suggest forthright and honest responding. In addition, the HTPP, KFD, and the TAT were administered according to protocol and are therefore also considered valid. Regarding the Rorschach Inkblot Test, the examiner had to depart significantly from standardized procedures to address Maura's defensiveness, and so the protocol is deemed invalid. The following results, therefore, do not include the Rorschach Inkblot Test.

Interpersonal Functioning:

Maura possesses several interpersonal strengths, including a friendly attitude, a desire for close relationships, and an altruistic tendency to reach out to others, particularly other young women. However, close interpersonal relationships tend to be problematic for her. She generally possesses a strong need for affection, but also maintains a suspicious attitude toward others that leads to marked difficulties with trust. She is likely to misperceive others' motives or actions and respond in a hypersensitive manner to any detected criticism or rejection. This interpretation of others' actions toward her may easily cause her to respond in an argumentative way of blaming them. Individuals with this tendency often use blaming as a means of self-protection or revenge. In Maura's cause, the history of abuse and trauma in her life has contributed significantly to the development of two intense needs: connection and affection with others, and personal safety. Her need for safety, then, causes social alienation or holding others at arm's length which leaves the need for affection unmet. This results in a self-defeating pattern where others end up reacting toward Maura in frustration or anger, which is exactly what she initially anticipates.

Coping and Stress:

Maura is a bright, competent, and driven individual who has successfully graduated college and attempts ambitious undertakings, such as writing and hoping to publish a book about her personal experiences in an attempt to help other women who are suffering. However, she has developed certain coping tendencies designed to ensure her personal safety, given the abuse she endured. The stress and fear caused by this abuse and the violence Maura has seen and experienced cause her to constantly check her environment for dangers to her physical and emotional well-being. Because this has always been her experience, it has likely been normalized, and therefore she may not be aware of either the intense level of stress and fear of the resulting hyper-vigilant disposition. Despite the chronic nature of stress and fear, Maura displays a coping strength in maintaining good physical health through a regular exercise regimen. Nonetheless, the data suggests that she also turns to certain compulsive and impulsive behaviors to achieve emotional relief under stress. Her history of anorexia constitutes this example of Maura's compulsive tendencies. With regard to impulsive action, in the past she has endorsed spontaneous decision making without forethought or planning. Overall, Maura is constantly managing a chronic and intense level of psychological distress.

Affect:

Maura's emotional life stems from her interpersonal history. Although Maura presents with a cheerful and pleasant disposition, there are indications that she experiences several long-standing underlying negative emotions including anger, depression, and anxiety. She tends to internalize emotions stemming from upsetting interpersonal experiences, which in turn culminates in a high level of resentment and anger. It appears that Maura does not adequately express her irritability or anger, and so her feelings "bottle up," so to speak, until they reach an uncontrollable level. Finally, the need Maura has to protect herself at all times produces a generally anxious temperament.

Self-Perception:

In terms of self-perception, Maura retains some degree of insecurity. She has absorbed some of the critical attitudes she often endured, and so she magnifies her flaws and sees herself as never good enough. In her tendency to anticipate criticism from others, Maura probably receives as true the negative comments directed toward her and generally interprets the comments of others through a negative filter. Yet the testing indicates that Maura is unable to accurately judge her many positive qualities. Furthermore, Maura struggles with being sensitive toward herself, probably expecting more from herself than she would reasonably expect from others.

RECOMMENDATIONS:

1. Due to the extensive trauma Maura has experienced, it is recommended that she engage in long-term, individual psychotherapy with a mental health professional trained to treat patients with trauma.

   A. Maura will likely benefit from a strong therapeutic alliance and interventions focused on the following:
      - Trauma resolution
      - Improving her ability to trust in interpersonal relationships
      - The development of adaptive coping skills
      - Efforts to help her establish a stable psychological identity

   B. Regarding trauma resolution, Maura will likely benefit from therapy to improve the clarity of her thinking, which involves sorting through her traumatic experiences.

   C. Additionally, therapeutic efforts to develop more healthy and adaptive expressions of anger are recommended for Maura.

2. *If Maura is going to engage in ongoing therapy to treat her trauma, it is suggested that she do so at a safe psychological and physical distance from the place and source of the trauma. Hence, she is likely to progress more quickly and effectively in therapy by leaving New Jersey.*

3. *Maura is likely to thrive in a work environment that is not reliant on the constant utilization of interpersonal skills and responding to interpersonal demands.*

    A. *Maura's work environment should not involve a high level of stress.*

    B. *Although Maura has a strong desire to reach out toward others in ministry, it is advisable that she ensure that she has a significant amount of reserved time and energy to address her own needs.*

4. *Lastly, it is recommended that Maura continue to work with a psychiatrist as well as maintain her regular method of exercise.*

When I left IPS I felt relieved that I finally knew I wasn't crazy and that I had a legitimate reason to feel what I was feeling. The doctors there were very kind and compassionate and helped me immensely, and for one of the first times in my life, I felt understood in regard to my mental health. I also felt extreme anger toward my dad. The abuse had caused so much pain, and I felt labeled as someone who had an eating disorder, depression, and a borderline personality disorder. I just wanted to be normal.

CHAPTER 11

Starting Over

The doctors advised me to leave New Jersey, go to trauma therapy, and essentially start a new life for myself. I was terrified but determined. One of the doctors at IPS told me about a Catholic psychologist in Nashville, Tennessee: Dr. William Bellet.

I called my friend Justina who lived in Nashville. I had met Justina during my time with FOCUS, and we had bonded over our love for Saint Padre Pio. I inquired about their housing situation and asked if I could move in with them. They had a full house, but she said she would let me know if anything changed. I started a novena to Saint Rita, patron saint of impossible causes, and called Dr. Bellet. I sent him my evaluation and then spoke with him again for ten minutes. He said he was confident that he could help me. On the last day of the novena, Justina called me and said one of their roommates had changed her mind and wasn't moving in. She said the room was mine if I wanted it. It was official—I was moving to Nashville! I was scared but peaceful at the same time.

Over the next few days I gathered up what I owned, and if it didn't fit in my Honda Accord, I gave it away. The hardest part about leaving was saying goodbye to Clare. I knew I would miss her greatly, but she was so incredibly supportive of the mission I was embarking on.

Like most siblings, Clare and I fought frequently growing up. We became best friends the later part of high school and in college and I'm so grateful we did. Clare is the most generous and loving woman. I always tell people that everyone needs a friend like Clare. She was the only one in my family to support me. Clare has a beautiful, Christlike heart. She has been with me through some of the darkest moments of my life. One attribute I love about Clare is her great ability to sit and listen to someone in pain without trying to fix the problem. Clare is one of the reasons I am alive today.

Clare and I have had countless adventures together. We have run hundreds of predawn runs together around the United States and world. We have run countless races together, been on many road trips, country music concerts, coffee shop dates, J.Crew shopping trips, beach and surfing adventures, study days in the Walsh Library at Seton Hall, and have cooked many meals together. We have always tried to keep Jesus at the center of our time together through going to Mass, adoration, and praying the Rosary and Divine Mercy Chaplet together. My friendship with Clare is a pure gift.

About halfway into my drive to Nashville, I thought I was going to have a panic attack. So many fearful thoughts kept racing through my mind. *What are you doing, Maura? Are you seriously moving to a state you've never even been to for a doctor you've never met? You don't have a job. You don't have health insurance. This is crazy.* I pulled over to the side of the road to let the negative thoughts pass and started praying the Rosary. Immediately I was flooded with immense peace. I knew in my heart that God was going to provide for me, but it was definitely scary to trust Him. I didn't see the whole picture, but He did.

The night before my first therapy session, I could barely sleep. I woke up early and went for a run in the hot southern heat. On my drive to Dr. Bellet's office, my mind churned furiously. *What if he can't help me? I mean, seriously, what good is this even going to do? Why did I think that telling a complete stranger everything that has happened to me is going to make me better? How could that take away the nightmares? What if he doesn't understand? And frankly, it's really none of his business anyway. Oh my gosh, did I make a mistake in moving here?*

Okay, calm down Maura. Trust in God—you have trusted Him to bring you here, and this is going to be no different. Take a deep breath. Breathe . . . everything is going to be okay. I knew in my heart this was what God wanted from me, but I was petrified, especially since the doctor was a man. I started praying the Rosary and arrived at his office.

He was late, and my mind used that as an excuse to try to run away. But I fought those thoughts with God's grace and remained seated in his waiting room. I'm glad I did, because even though I was shaking, by the end of the two-hour session, I knew God had placed Dr. Bellet in my life as a tremendous gift. As soon as I closed his office door, I bowed my head in grateful thanksgiving.

Therapy was incredibly exhausting, grueling, and intense, and that day, I promised myself I would never give up. No matter how hard it got, I would keep going back. One time I did tell Dr. Bellet I couldn't come back because it was too hard, but that was just my frustration speaking. I went back again and again.

My third session was exceedingly challenging, and when I left his office that afternoon, I couldn't stop crying. *This is so hard! I don't know how I'm going to make it through. I'm just not that strong—how am I going to do this?* Later that day I went to Adoration and decided that I was going to offer up each session and homework activity for my future children. I desperately yearned for my future children to not have to suffer from the ramifications of abuse.

So, when therapy seemed unbearable, or I had to draw or describe events and body parts that I thought I would never be able to do, I would close my eyes and picture what my future children might look like. I imagined their tiny hands and their ten little toes and how I desired to surround them with love and tenderness. I thought about all that I would want to teach them about God the Father, Jesus, Mary, and the saints. Then I thought about how strong I would need to be for them and how much I needed to grow and heal before I could get married and have children. I thought about my wedding day and buying a wedding dress. I thought about walking down the aisle toward my husband. Then I opened my eyes gently, as I opened my doctor's office door and proceeded to another therapy session.

While in therapy I learned that receiving appropriate love is very important. It allows the giver to get out of themselves and think of another. Therefore, I realized that when I turned down a perfectly genuine gesture of love from a friend, it brought the attention to me, instead of focusing on the giver who was trying to do a kind act. So in reality, when I receive love from others, I am allowing the giver to grow in virtue and character, and I, the receiver, am growing too. I am learning to trust again, which is exceedingly challenging after trauma, when people have let me down, or when I constantly question others' motives. So in therapy, every time I firmly shook someone's hand or focused on making eye contact with them, they had no idea all that I was practicing. Everyday tasks that come as second nature to some became a monument achievement for me.

Here is a look inside my therapy journal to give you an example of some of my fears, challenges, and the areas I desired to grow in.

July 7, 2010

Fear of not being good enough for marriage. Fear that someone I marry will abuse me, use me, and then leave me. Fear of running away and not facing my past. Fear of thinking Charlie's pornography addiction was my fault. Fear of thinking I'm not pretty enough. Fear that I could never satisfy someone in a relationship and marriage.

I need to challenge myself not to overthink things and offer my cross to God. I want to love my cross. Jesus, please help me to love my cross.

July 14, 2010:

I really like going to talk to Dr. Bellet; it really helps me. I like that he listens to me. I feel better after seeing him, even though the pain is deep. I know this is going to be really hard and a lot of work, but with God's grace I can do it.

July 15, 2010:

Everything hurts so much; I'm not sure if I can do this. I had no idea how hard therapy was going to be. I am really overwhelmed. It just hurts everywhere, and my nightmares are intense.

I was in Starbucks, and something I saw there triggered a bad memory. My eyes welled up with tears, but I was determined not to let it ruin the rest of my day. The only thing to do is to trust in God and move forward.

I keep having so many bad dreams.

Oct 7, 2010:

Things to work on: confidence, self-image, looking people straight in the eyes, giving people a firm handshake and focusing on their eyes, letting people stand and or sit close to me "in my space."

I don't need to be afraid to talk about the abuse. I did nothing wrong.

March 13, 2011:

"You don't have to be afraid of the things you were afraid of when you were five" (from the movie The King's Speech)

So I wrote a list of the things that I'm afraid of:
   1) men in general;
   2) waking up in the middle of the night to horrible nightmares;
   3) the police;
   4) yelling and screaming;

5) harsh words;

6) anything rough;

7) anything sexual.

May 26, 2011:

Dr. Bellet is such a gift, and I'm so grateful for him. I really feel God's love through this gift He has given me.

July 12, 2011:

I feel a lot more hopeful and joyful lately. I feel like I have part of my life back, and it feels wonderful. I still have hard days, but I honestly feel like a new person. I don't feel depressed anymore, and I love how that feels. I can go out and have fun with my friends and not be so fearful. I am still working hard in therapy, and I don't know when I'll be done, but it feels so great to be finally feeling better.

I want to be a saint and need to pray more for the grace to be one. I want to love those who have hurt me and show them the love of the Father. I want to show them His mercy. I want to be an instrument of His love. I desire for those who have never had an encounter with the Father to feel His love through me. Father, please help me to always act in such a way that I will demonstrate your love to all of those with whom I come in contact.

I need to pray more for the grace to offer my suffering to Christ, so as to be a co-redeemer with Him. I also need to pray more for the grace to be joyful and bask in His hope always.

July 13, 2011:

Dr. Bellet isn't going to hurt me, and I can tell him anything. I really think I can trust him.

July 20, 2011:

Look in the mirror today and say "**I am enough**" ten times out loud. Visualize it.

Think it. Believe it. Live it.

August 24, 2011:

Working hard on looking people in the eyes and giving people firm handshakes to build up my confidence. Continuing to work on getting out of myself and trying to focus on what others may be thinking or feeling.

The other night, after returning from a long day of work, my roommates said they would love it if I would join them for dinner. Instead of focusing on me and how much I just wanted to go to bed, I ate with them and thought about them and what they wanted. Sometimes I can't believe people want to spend time with me.

I practiced saying the words sex *and* pornography *over and over again and tried to get a little louder each time. I remember when I couldn't even say them or when Dr. Bellet would say them and I would start to cry. I guess I am making progress.*

I didn't refuse an invitation to go on a date.

I relived an exceedingly painful memory when I saw something that triggered the memory, and I prayed for the grace to see beauty in the pain. In the past, I would have just started to cry; instead of focusing on my own pain, I focused on others.

Dr. Bellet gave me another exercise to do during therapy, and it really helped me:

Three Gratitudes—write three new things each day for which you are grateful. Do this every day for twenty-one days in a row.

Journaling—write every day about one positive experience you've had or something good that happened to you over the past twenty-four hours.

Exercise—every day, even just a brisk walk to get your heart rate going and something to build strength in one or more muscle groups. The key is not how much or how long but consistency— every day for a full twenty-one days.

Meditation (or prayer)—spend five minutes, but no more than ten or fifteen minutes, every day in conversation with God. Start by telling Him how much you love Him and then share your thoughts (positive or negative) as though you are talking to a good friend.

Random Acts of Kindness—tell someone or write and send one positive thing praising someone for what they do well or for how they please you.

Each week when I was in therapy, my doctor had me write a list of positive things from the week as part of my homework. He wanted me to focus on the positive things instead of dwelling on my pain, and this really helped me cultivate a spirit of gratitude.

1. *I looked at myself in the mirror and said out loud: "I'm a daughter of God, created in His image and likeness. I am beautiful because my dignity flows from Him. He doesn't create ugly."*
2. *A guy at work put his hand on my shoulder and asked me on a date. It made me feel really uncomfortable, but I tried not to overreact and to just relax. Seriously, why couldn't he have just asked me out without touching me?*
3. *I've been on several dates with John. It's actually been fun to date him. (I can see you smiling right now, Dr. Bellet).*
4. *I tried to be more assertive at work. I did this by not asking what people thought, but instead was confident in my ability as a baker. And I was so proud of myself when I did because the head chef said my biscotti were the best he had ever eaten.*
5. *I didn't lock my bedroom door this week, although I was really tempted to.*
6. *I went running during the day. This guy rolled down his window and whistled at me. Gosh, I hate that—it's so annoying. I tried really hard not to let it bother me, but instead just let it roll off my shoulder.*
7. *I went swimming and wore a bathing suit.*

8. *I wore a sleeveless shirt without feeling self-conscious.*

9. *I saw my reflection in a window and saw God's beauty, instead of the ugliness I have usually seen.*

10. *I decided after three years of being a slave to the effects of Charlie's addiction to pornography that I wasn't going to let it have a hold on me anymore. His addiction wasn't my fault, and I am beautiful. I am worth being pursued.*

11. *I thought about how far I've come from college and thanked God for my progress.*

12. *I remember in college that it was hard for me to wear shorts or short sleeves because I was so self-conscious after Charlie's addiction. And I never wore my hair down because I knew some people would find it attractive, and I didn't want anyone looking at me. But I did all of those things this week, and it felt so good.*

13. *One night during the week, I woke up from a bad nightmare and thought I heard somebody in my room. I got up and looked around my room and told myself that it was just a dream. And I didn't even lock my door; I was so proud of myself.*

14. *I tried really hard to look directly into someone's eyes when I shook their hand. I also gave them a firm handshake.*

15. *One of the guys at work saw me lifting a fifty-pound bag of flour and offered to help me. My natural inclination was to say, "I got it," because let's be real, I did. But I thought about what Dr. Bellet said about letting people, especially men, help me, so I said, "Thank you, that would be great."*

16. *I'm getting more used to physical touch. One of the girls at work gave me a really tight hug, and it felt so good.*

17. *I let my roommate braid my hair because I had accidentally sliced my finger at work and couldn't braid my hair. It didn't hurt to let her touch my hair, it actually felt good to let someone help me.*

18. *I chose to continue to choose forgiveness.*

19. *Someone once told me, "The depth of our love is how well we receive it." I never used to be able to receive love from people. I always questioned their motives. Why does this person want to help me?*

Why are they being so nice to me? They couldn't possibly mean what they say. How could they love me? I feel so unlovable; they must want something in return. I mean, really, what is it that they want from me? I think about these things a lot. While it is still difficult at times to trust, especially when it comes to men and relationships, I have made great progress. I am so grateful for God the Father's love in my life and His hand over me. He wants my good.

CHAPTER 12

Beginning Therapy

*A*nother thing that was very healing for me during therapy was learning about God's intent for sex and its goodness within the sacrament of marriage.

Science proves that breaking up from a sexual relationship is more difficult than a nonsexual relationship. When a man and woman have sex, there are many chemical processes that take place. The brain produces dopamine during sex, which is an exceedingly powerful chemical. Dopamine is responsible for internal pleasure, and when a man and woman have sex, it produces a bond that is not easily forgotten.

Oxytocin is also produced in great quantities, which is a very strong hormone produced mainly in women when they have sex, give birth, and breastfeed their babies. This is why sex is for bonding and babies and why mothers have such a profound bond with their babies. Oxytocin is also one of the reasons why a woman will stay with a man who is abusing her, because she is literally bonded to him.

The chemical that bonds a man to a woman is vasopressin, and it has the same effect as oxytocin. This is why God designed sex for marriage, because it literally binds a husband and wife together. One might pose the question: "Well, I think I'm going to marry him or her anyway, so we might as well have sex, right?"

Wrong.

When you have sex, you are bonding with your partner, therefore disrupting the discernment process. Sex will unite you together regardless, and this is why there is so much heartache in our society today. One of the reasons why one-night stands never work is that after sex, there is an emotional attachment, but no lifelong commitment.

One of the greatest treasures Saint John Paul II left to the world is his series of audiences called *Theology of the Body*. He talks about the human person and explains how God is made manifested through humanity. *Theology of the Body* delves into what it truly means to be a man and woman, our sexuality, and how we should live out our masculinity and femininity in accord with how God created us. If we yearn to be the best version of ourselves, then we must embrace the unique qualities of our gender. To do this we must go back to the very beginning when God created us. Genesis 1:27 tells us: "God created man in his own image, in the image of God he created him; male and female he created them."

God created us out of love, for us to love and be loved. The way in which this love is expressed and revealed is different for men and women, which is how God in His infinite wisdom designed it to be. And it is the unique characteristics of men and women that enable this love to come to fruition. We exist to complement one another, a man as the pursuer and the woman as the receiver. In *Theology of the Body*, Saint John Paul II tells us that we are called to exist as a gift for one another. He describes this gift as a sincere gift of self, and it is only when we lay down our life for another in this way that we will experience genuine fulfillment.

In order to understand God's plan for humanity in our fallen world, we must go back to the beginning and see what God intended for us. It is only when we do this that we will be filled with hope and peace. In the beginning of time after God created the world, He saw that it wasn't good for man to be alone; thus

He created woman. Eve was created as a sincere gift for Adam, and Adam as a gift for her. They were created to complement one another in their union, each to offer themselves to the other as a gift.

Our society today has lost sight of this quintessential ideal due to selfishness. Our culture is plagued with violence and unrest due to a hook-up mentality, impurity, lack of self-control and virtue, pornography, and a genuine lack of respect for the dignity of the human person.

Discovering these truths played a tremendous role in my healing. I had the privilege of having spiritual direction after college from Monsignor John Esseff. Monsignor Esseff is a diocesan priest in Scranton, Pennsylvania. He has served as a confessor to Saint Teresa of Kolkata and the Missionaries of Charity. He also encountered St. Padre Pio, who bilocated to him. Saint Pio became a spiritual father to him.

I used to go to Pennsylvania to visit Monsignor Esseff for spiritual direction. During one visit, he told me, "We are closest to Christ when we feel rejected, isolated, and alone, because this is what Jesus felt in the Garden of Gethsemane." Another time during spiritual direction he said to me, "I can see it—Mary and Jesus are right next to you in your suffering."

One night when it was time for me to leave after spiritual direction, he said, "Hold on, I have something for you." He went to his room while I waited downstairs near the chapel. He returned several minutes later with a picture of Padre Pio I had never seen before. "Wow, I love it!" I said. "Where did you get that? I've never seen this picture of him before."

"Padre Pio gave it to me to give to you," he said. I got the chills. Monsignor Esseff looked at me one last time that night and said, "One day you will see. One day you will have an army behind you." I didn't understand what he meant and contemplated his words on my drive home.

I could see that even in my darkest moments, God the Father had never left me; He was closest to me in those moments. We are forged in our suffering, and Jesus will never leave us alone, even though it might feel like we are alone.

These were Monsignor Esseff's words to me that day:

Isolation: Jesus was isolated in the Garden of Gethsemane. Talk to God when you feel alone.

Rejection: You are closest to God when you are rejected. Love is the greatest force in the world. If the most significant person in your life lets you down, who do you turn to? You turn to God the Father, who understands your pain.

Abandonment: *Jesus was abandoned. He experienced Pilot condemning Him when He was innocent. You are Jesus, so pray to God the Father, just as He did.*

Monsignor Esseff also said to stop saying "I" and replace it with "You." *You (Heavenly Father) let me see that by being resentful, I am destroying myself and not those who have hurt and abused me. You let me see the beauty You see. You teach me how to receive love. You teach me to let go. You teach me to trust. You teach me to hope. You teach me to love.*

I worked many jobs to pay for the care that I needed, working up to three jobs at a time for a year. It was a tremendous amount of work, but a good kind of work, the kind of work that makes you feel proud for accomplishing something. I had to pay for therapy, my medication (which was two hundred dollars a bottle) and my psychiatrist appointments. People were also very generous to me. One week I went to see Dr. Bellet for three sessions during a month when money was so tight. When I went to pay him, he told me the sessions were on him and to just keep working hard. One of my roommates helped me with my rent for over a year, which was extraordinarily generous.

One month I took a second job selling health and life insurance. I sat in class for weeks that summer and spent many of my Friday evenings at Starbucks, studying all of the state and nationwide laws in relation to insurance. September came, and I passed my tests for certification.

I never dreamed that I'd be an insurance agent; it's so opposite my personality. But I was determined to make sure I was able to afford the care I needed. So there I was in the world of pinstriped suits, high heels, and leather briefcases, chatting with co-workers at the office who read the *Wall Street Journal* every morning with their grande skinny lattes.

As the months passed, I realized that I couldn't in good conscience stay with the company. One Friday night I came home from meeting with clients all day and was really distraught. The insurance company was shady, and I didn't feel comfortable working for my boss. I had inquired about baking jobs all over Nashville, but I couldn't even get an interview because I had no professional culinary experience.

A few months prior I had catered the desserts at my brother's rehearsal dinner in San Diego. During the event, the photographer approached me and told me my carrot cake was one of the best he had ever eaten. He has shot weddings around the world and his work is published in countless wedding magazines, so I believed he was being genuine.

I grew up baking and cooking and had always wanted to be a baker. My mom had a great gift of bringing people together through her cooking, and I learned a lot by watching her. So that Friday night I came home, took off my heels and suit, put on some comfy running clothes, wiped the makeup off my face, and sat down at our kitchen table to come up with a game plan. *Maybe I can't get a job interview because I have no professional culinary experience, but maybe I can get a job once they've tried my food.*

I made a list of all the desserts and breakfast foods people had told me they really enjoyed. My plan was to go to the store and buy ingredients, stay up until 5:00 a.m. to bake, sleep until 7:00 a.m., add the finishing touches on all the baked goods until 10:00 a.m., package and load everything into my car, and then go around Nashville to all the places I wanted to work and give each manager a sample of my food along with a business card.

Although I knew it would be a challenge to accomplish all that I had planned with one oven and no Kitchen Aid mixer, I knew I could do it. So, with some good music playing thanks to Pandora, I began. Everything was out of the oven by 5:30 a.m., and I slept until 7:00 a.m. My roommates were fairly used to my "adventures" and woke up to an array of baked goods on our kitchen table and counters.

I made business cards and boxed up my baked goods and went to all of the restaurants and cafes I wanted to work at. I asked for the manager and gave them a box of my baked goods. The next week, I got six job offers. And that is how my baking career started.

For months when I was in therapy, I tried to say, "I'm a survivor," but couldn't. I didn't feel like a survivor. I felt trapped in pain, horrific memories, ragging nightmares, and feelings that I couldn't articulate. During one particular therapy session, Dr. Bellet said, "Here, Maura, I have something I think you will like." Sitting in his leather chair, he swiveled closer to his desk, opened his laptop and inserted a CD. As he pressed play, I heard Saint John Paul II recite the following in English, coupled with his pronounced Polish accent: "Do not be afraid. Do not be satisfied with mediocrity. Put out into the deep and let down your nets for a catch." What pierced my heart were the words, "Be not afraid." His deep yet gentle voice provoked a sense of safety and peacefulness in my soul.

His words inspired me to fight harder for freedom, as they fostered a deeper urge to combat evil with beauty. As the months passed, the evil I was terrified to talk about slowly surfaced through dialogue with my doctor in a safe setting. As I revealed more to him, the effects of the abuse slowly unraveled. At first I thought that if I told Dr. Bellet, it would be wrong and that someone was going to get in trouble. Through prayer, God revealed to me His beautiful plan and the depths of His fatherly love. I came to the conclusion that if I held the abuse inside, it had the potential to control the rest of my life. *Why should I punish myself any longer for something that wasn't even my fault?* I used to blame myself, but I came to the realization of just how twisted my thought process was. I needed to reshape my thought process, and I knew in my heart that my doctor could help me.

Was I scared to take that leap of faith and trust my doctor? Was I scared to step out into the water, trusting that the Father would catch me? You bet I was. But what scared me more was being complacent—that terrified me. I was in the care of a phenomenal doctor. If I let the opportunity pass, I would be living a mediocre life. And Saint John Paul II specifically said, "Do not be satisfied with mediocrity."

I wasn't about to let that happen. I wanted to get married and have a family. I wanted to live in freedom. I was determined to fight until I could confidently say, "I'm a survivor" *and truly believe it.* My doctor made me a copy of that CD, and in the months that followed, I used it daily to practice enunciating words, phrases, and life experiences that I couldn't say on my own. I needed someone else's voice to surmount mine so I wouldn't hear what I was saying. I would turn on the CD and listen to the sound of Saint John Paul II's voice. Then I would turn up the volume, so his voice overpowered mine. Over time, I was able to turn down the CD, so my voice resounded above his. I still couldn't confidently say, "I'm a survivor," but my doctor told me to just let it come out naturally.

As I practiced living in gratitude, I became very aware of how God the Father had provided for me through therapy. I desired to take the gift I had been given and help others find similar healing in their lives. I wrestled with the idea of starting a nonprofit to help women.

A year passed, and when I neared the end of therapy, I met with an accountant about my idea to start a nonprofit. He asked me why I wanted to do this, and I confidently looked him straight in the eyes and said, "I'm a survivor." It flowed so naturally, and for a second I couldn't believe what I had just said. I smiled—and my smile was huge.

Later that evening I went before the Lord in the Blessed Sacrament. I thanked Him for the gift He had given me through my doctor, the Cross, and the potential of Made in His Image. There was no one else praying, so I knelt as close to the Tabernacle as I could, and said it aloud again, "I'M A SURVIVOR!"

During my time in therapy, I really tried to put into practice what Dr. Burns had taught me about forgiveness in Colorado a few years prior. Forgiveness doesn't excuse another person's behavior; forgiveness prevents their behavior from destroying you. Forgiveness, just like love, is a choice. Every day when I prayed, I asked God for the grace to forgive my dad. I prayed for the grace to forgive my mom for not protecting me and for being so manipulative. Her gaslighting tendencies were very hurtful, but they taught me to set up healthy boundaries to protect myself. I also had to forgive myself for holding on to so much shame and for blaming myself for the abuse. This was incredibly hard. I read Henri Nouwen's book, *The Return of the Prodigal Son*, and this book transformed my life.

In 1669 the Dutch painter Rembrandt van Rijn painted his greatest work shortly before his death, and this artwork is on the cover of Henri Nouwen's book. *The Return of the Prodigal Son* taught me that at one point in our life we are all like the "prodigal son" who squanders his inheritance and lives a sinful life through lust and selfishness. We can also see ourselves at one point or another as the "second son" who is with the father but is bursting with anger and resentment. We are all called to become the father; we are called to love like he loves. God the Father doesn't want to leave us in sinfulness and resentment. He wants to bring us to new life.

Oftentimes our perception of God the Father is a reflection of our relationship with our earthly father, which is sad because so many of us come from broken homes with an abusive or absent father. One of the most comforting and striking aspects of Rembrandt's painting is the variation in the size of the father's hands. The right hand is smaller, more slender, and exudes gentleness. The left hand is larger, more defined, and reveals great strength. The differences in the size of the hands captures both the masculine and feminine expression of love. This appealed to my heart in a beautiful and healing way, showing me that God the Father is both powerful and gentle.

CHAPTER 13

Healing Journey

I n April 2011, Dr. Bellet recommended I see the movie *There Be Dragons* that was playing in select movie theaters. Set during the Spanish Civil War, it tells the story of St. Josemaría Escrivá and his childhood friend, Manolo Torres. As the two lads mature, they both enter the seminary. Josemaría answers God's call and becomes a Catholic priest, eventually founding the Opus Dei (Work of God) movement. After leaving the seminary himself, Manolo becomes a spy for the fascists.

As hatred, betrayal, and jealousy escalate throughout the movie for Manolo, he becomes a slave to his anger. As a Catholic priest fighting for his life, Josemaría chooses to spread seeds of hope and forgiveness. On one particular occasion, while Josemaría and his priests were hiding for their lives in a psychiatric hospital, a beautiful redheaded woman approaches him and shows him the scars on her wrists, where she had cut herself. Petrified with fear, she tells him, "I was raped and still sleep with the lights on. I lock my door at night and put a chair under the door handle." Gentle tears rolled down my face as she continued to say, "I have accepted that God can be terrible. And now my prayers are deeper. I fight Him with love."

My heart almost pounded out of my chest. Her courage was inspiring and her innocence radiated true beauty as she said gently yet firmly, "I fight Him with love." This woman had suffered immensely, but her response to suffering was courageous and beautiful. She was one of the most minor characters in the movie, yet her reply, "I fight Him with love," made her one of the most compelling. I wanted to be like her.

After the movie, I created a blog that I didn't think anyone would read. I called it *I Fight Him with Love*. I loved the redheaded woman's response to suffering. This woman knew that God allowed evil to happen because of man's fallen nature, but instead of turning inward and focusing on her own resentment, anger, and hate, she chose to focus outward and make the choice to love. She chose to fight her anger with love, mercy, and forgiveness, and that's what I wanted to do.

Much to my surprise, people did read my blog. One night I wrote an entry about my dream of starting a nonprofit. The next day I got an email from a gentleman who wanted to help me financially. I was shocked and so excited. We met for pizza and wine and talked about many things. At the end of the dinner he handed me a check for three thousand dollars, the exact amount I had been praying for. I knew my ministry was God's will because I hadn't given him a number, but I had done the calculations and three thousand dollars was what I needed to start my ministry. When God wants something to happen, He will pave a way even when it seems daunting.

In therapy I learned that when faced with suffering, you have two choices—you can love, or you can hate. You can combat the person or situation with the love and mercy of the Father, or you can hold a grudge and let the anger deteriorate you. The choice is yours.

The day after I started my blog, I got a late-night call from my friend Molly. I knew something was wrong by the sound of her voice. She said she needed to go to the ER. I jumped out of bed, threw on my jeans, grabbed my keys, and headed out the door. Molly then said she could go by herself. I told her I wouldn't let her and asked her to let me love her by taking her.

I started praying the Rosary as I drove to her house, but I got distracted by the decades and just prayed Hail Marys. I didn't know what I would find when I got there, and I was nervous. We packed up her things, got in my car, and drove to the ER. Once inside, the nurse asked her various questions, and we were taken to a stretcher in the hallway, as the ER rooms were already full. It was 10:00 p.m.

Molly was severely struggling with an eating disorder, and the attending physician said it would be hours before the psychiatrist would be able to give her a consult. We decided to make the most of our time there and played music from Molly's laptop. We let the nurses bring us heated blankets as they made jokes about who the patient was, since we were both sitting on the stretcher. One of the nurses thought for sure we had coordinated our visits to the ER, and we joked back saying there was seriously no other place we would rather be at 2:00 a.m. But as vitals were taken and blood drawn, we knew the severity of the visit.

So we didn't just joke around; we got serious. We both knew why we were there, and the pain was a little too familiar for both of us. Molly asked me questions about how I was recovering, and I told her. We cried together.

The psychiatrist finally came to see Molly at 3:30 a.m. I walked into the waiting room so they could talk. I tried to sit quietly but pacing felt more comfortable. I paced the waiting room for a while, cried a little, and then sat down. My heart really ached for Molly.

She called me when they were done, and I walked into the ER again. It was 4:10 a.m. This time we really got serious in our conversation. She asked me to share one of the turning points in my recovery. And I told her.

I was sitting in a quiet church, holding on to my eating disorder with every ounce of strength within me. Then I gave it to God, and I mean, I really gave it to God. I told Him I wanted to be healthy. I told Him I wanted to be the weight He wanted me to be. I told Him I wanted to feel His love. I told Him I would put away the scale and trust in Him. I told God I would eat even when I might not be hungry. I told God I needed His grace to not binge eat again. I told Him I would keep going to therapy and taking my medication.

"Were you scared?" Molly asked.

"I was scared out of my mind," I replied.

I told her my thought process. God gives us all free will, but He desperately wants us to choose Him. He wants us to make the right choice, eating three meals a day, not abusing exercise, not purging and binging. But He can't force us to make that choice. We have to want it. I told her that everyone needs to make that choice for themselves. God is waiting right next to us, hoping we choose Him, but He isn't going to force us. I told her that talking about the trauma in therapy was actually diminishing my eating disorder, as weird as that may sound.

Dr. Bellet was the one who inspired me to launch my nonprofit, Made in His Image. Toward the end of my journey in therapy, he said, "Everyone suffers. But it is what we do with our sufferings that will make us a saint."

That night he sent me this email:

Seek beauty in all things. To embrace love, you must see what is beautiful. Watching you struggle today and succeed was a great thing of beauty for me to behold. Your precious journal is and remains beautiful. It has in it your deepest thoughts and feelings, dried tears, smudges, corrections, sketches, and the like—verses and paintings of love and pain. This is life. Never throw out your memories, but instead turn the ugly ones back into what God intended them to be. Only when you need to purge, write or draw things on pieces of scrap paper that you can burn immediately. However, even then, as you watch the billowing smoke rise, ask God to receive what is painful and to supply you with what is beautiful and peaceful. You will never be able to replace and exchange yourself, your body, your experiences, or your memories for anything else. God made you and will make everything that you and others do into something good and beautiful. Keep your book; treasure it and envision its old and tattered state over time—a personal guide of your journey and your personal attempt to turn all things that He has given to you into a treasure. Let God turn things to dust as He will do with all things (and from which He created all things). God is God, and we are not.

Made in His Image is both a ministry and a nonprofit, helping women of all ages who are suffering from eating disorders, depression, anxiety, or physical and/or sexual abuse to find psychological, spiritual, and emotional healing. I am passionate about uncovering the shroud of silence associated with mental health and therapy. My ultimate dream with Made in His Image is to build the first Catholic inpatient and outpatient medical center for women recovering from eating disorders and abuse.

Through my work with Made in His Image, I have traveled to Belize and Uganda and have given hundreds of talks in the United States. One of my main goals through my work with Made in His Image is to help women know that they aren't alone and that living in recovery is possible. I want them to feel God the Father's message of hope through my words and presence on social media.

When I was leaving my last session of therapy, I felt like Will from the movie *Good Will Hunting*. *What do I do when I'm face-to-face with the doctor who changed my life? What do I say? What words could there possibly be to describe the depth of my gratitude?* At that moment, I realized I could never compose a string of words to describe my appreciation to Dr. Bellet, so I remained silent and spoke the deepest words from my heart by smiling and extending my right hand to shake his, something I had never done throughout our journey together. I was always so afraid to get physically close to men that even shaking hands was difficult.

I left Dr. Bellet's office and entered the elevator. As I descended, I was in awe that I had actually completed all of the sessions. You know that feeling you get when you have worked so hard to achieve something and then the final moment of completion arrives? That's how it felt, coupled with countless other emotions.

As I got off the elevator, I just stood there in shock. An impulse reaction took over, and I got back in the elevator. My index finger automatically pushed the button for the fifth floor, as I had pushed hundreds of times before. I knocked on Dr. Bellet's office door. He said, "Come in." He stood up and, with tears in my eyes, I hugged him. "Thank you for changing my life." Tears formed in his eyes as he said, "It was an honor to help you." I'll never forget that moment.

After completing two and a half years of intense trauma therapy, I learned that:

1. There are doctors that genuinely care and understand. They might not have experienced the same difficulties you have, but they are trained extensively to help you. It takes tremendous faith and trust on your part to be vulnerable with them.

2. There are countless ways to express your pain and struggles. It will take time, but you can start slowly and build up to revealing more. You can also draw or paint to express your feelings, traumas, and emotions. Art therapy helped me tremendously. I remember drawing certain images that I couldn't describe with words, and afterward Dr. Bellet burned those images for me. It was really healing.

3. I worked six days a week in the beginning to pay for the care I needed, often working three jobs to cover my expenses. I was awestruck at the generosity of my doctors who made

my care affordable for me. One psychiatrist never sent me a bill for two thousand dollars. When I went to pay the receptionist, she told me, "In his twenty-five years of practice I have never seen him not bill a patient. I don't know who you are, but you don't owe us anything." People genuinely want to help, and it was healing for my wounded heart to receive love through others generosity.

4. It's okay to be scared; it's normal. When I first met my doctor, I was terrified. I knew in my heart God wanted me to take this leap of faith. Over time I learned to trust Dr. Bellet. It was healing for me to learn that there are people in the world who are deserving of my trust.

5. As I healed, I learned that it didn't matter if my family found out I was in therapy. This was my life, and it was time for me to stand up for myself and own my healing. If I didn't go to therapy, I would be living my life in fear, and this isn't what God wanted for me. Jesus came to shine a light in the darkness, and abuse needs to be out in the open. Left in the dark, it festers and destroys lives, and it needs to be exposed as the evil it is.

6. In 2010 I sat in Arlington, Virginia, at the Institute for the Psychological Sciences (IPS) when Dr. Kathryn Benes compared me to a soldier returning from war. Dr. Benes was the director of the Catholic-based Psychology Ministry at Catholic Charities in the Archdiocese of Denver. Prior to moving to Colorado, she served as an associate professor and director of the training clinic at the Institute for the Psychological Sciences. Dr. Benes also developed a nationally recognized, diocesan-wide mental health program that ultimately became a doctoral-level psychology internship site in the Nebraska Internship Consortium in Psychology, an institution accredited by the American Psychological Association (APA). This program is currently the only APA-

accredited internship site in the nation that is specifically designed to train psychologists from a Catholic perspective.

Seeing Dr. Benes' credentials and hearing what she said about me helped reshape my thought process. My brother was a captain in the United States Marine Corps and served two missions overseas, and if I knew he needed help, I would encourage him to get it. I would definitely not think he was weak for getting help. I would think he was tremendously courageous for embracing what needs to be dealt with, instead of simply ignoring it.

Why didn't I see myself as worthy of the same care? Why wasn't I good enough to receive help? I wrestled with these thoughts and came to discover my dignity as God's daughter worthy of care. God the Father desired nothing more than to provide, protect and take care of me in my brokenness. He just wanted me to trust Him. Will you not let Him provide for you the same way?

CHAPTER 14

A Move to California

In the fall of 2011, I saw FOCUS' new missions video and really connected with it. The man in the video talked about his experience in Kolkata, India—the same mission trip I had been on. He talked about how he developed a deeper relationship with God the Father on the trip and how it took going to India to find his identity as God's son.

I reached out to FOCUS on their Facebook page and they put me in touch with the videographer, Michael Preszler. I reached out to Michael with a quick message on Facebook: *Hey, I saw your video for FOCUS missions and really loved it! I'm looking for a videographer for a project I'm starting. Do you do work outside of FOCUS?*

A few days later Michael messaged me back saying he was interested, but that he was in the process of moving to New York City from Denver, Colorado. He said if I was ever in New York City to give him a call.

I messaged him a few weeks later saying that I was going to be in New Jersey for a meeting in February and that if it worked for us to get together, that would be awesome. In February 2012, Michael messaged me saying that if I could come into the city, we could share a meal together and talk about the video.

I love New York City and took the train in from New Jersey one night. Michael met me at Penn Station, and we walked to a quaint Italian restaurant. I think because it wasn't a date, I felt really comfortable. I had been on several dates with a guy I really liked in Nashville, and Michael told me that he was on a dating fast. I shared a little about Made in His Image and what I was looking for in a promotional video. Michael shared about how he got started in videography. We talked about our trips to India, and it was neat to have that connection. After all, you don't meet many people who have been to Saint Mother Teresa's home for the dying, where we both had served.

After dinner, Michael invited me back to his apartment, which he shared with several other FOCUS missionaries. He offered me some tea and we talked some more. He was really easy to converse with. After about an hour I said I needed to get back to Penn Station, and he offered to walk with me. The video ended up not working out due to our locations, though, and we didn't stay in touch.

When I finished therapy and launched Made in His Image, I started giving talks. I have always loved San Diego, California, and was very excited when a woman named Carrie from Saint Brigid parish in Pacific Beach, California, reached out to me to see if I was available to give a talk in August 2013 to the young adult community she worked with. At first I thought the trip wasn't going to work out because, while they were going to compensate me for my talk, I had to cover my own airfare. But then I thought the trip would be a great opportunity for my ministry, so I redeemed some airfare miles and booked my flight.

The trip was amazing—I had so much fun! The morning after my talk I met up with Carrie for coffee and we chatted for a while. Toward the end, I casually mentioned that I really wanted to move to San Diego, and she said she would talk to a few people about housing situations if I wanted. On my flight back to Nashville I prayed a Rosary that God would show me where he wanted me next. I went to Adoration when I got back and gave the Lord my heart. I knew I had moved to Nashville to go to therapy, but I was done with therapy now. *But what if something were to happen and I needed to go back to therapy? What would I do then?* I told Jesus that if he wanted me to move to San Diego, He would need to provide.

I had just signed a lease several months ago with three women, and I loved our beautiful home. I would need someone to take my room, and I would need to find a job and housing in San Diego. I applied for several baking jobs in San Diego and told several friends that I was looking for someone to take over my room and rent. Within days, I got several job interviews in San Diego and a friend took my room. I called Carrie and she put me in touch with her best friend, Kristin, who was looking for a roommate. I flew back to California for some job interviews and met with Kristin. God worked it out beautifully—I got the baking job I really wanted, and Kristin said she would love to have me as a roommate.

My incredible friends in Nashville threw me an amazing going-away party, and I felt so loved. Dr. Bellet came, too, which was really special to me. It was bittersweet to leave Nashville. Nashville felt like home to me, but I knew in my heart it was time to move on. It was time to step outside of my comfort zone and continue to place my trust in God for my future. He had brought me so far, and I knew He had an amazing plan for me in San Diego too. And indeed He did.

A week later I packed up my Honda Accord and left for San Diego. I was excited but nervous. Everything in Nashville had become so comfortable to me. I knew my group of friends so well and loved them so much. We had the best adventures, with lots of porch and margarita nights together. The hardest part was saying goodbye to Dr. Bellet. Even though I knew I didn't need therapy, it was comforting just knowing he was there. He had become a father figure to me, and I was going to miss him very much. It's always hard moving to a new city and starting over again, but I tried to focus on the positive, and I knew in my heart this move was providentially arranged by God.

It was a twenty-four-hour drive from Nashville to San Diego. I really enjoy driving by myself, and I had plenty of time to listen to music, pray, and ponder all that the Lord had done for me. As I was driving through Texas, I was moved to tears thinking about all the ways God's hand had touched my life in such a profound way. I was filled with gratitude, from my time with Varsity Catholic, the mission trip to India, Eric teaching me about God the Father's love, my holy hours with Jesus in the Blessed Sacrament, Dr. Burns teaching me through his witness about forgiveness, my time at IPS, my move to Nashville and how God used Dr. Bellet to change my life. I know it sounds so cliché when someone says, "My life was changed." But my life truly was changed through therapy.

Before therapy I felt like I was half there. I didn't feel free. I had so much confusion, anger, pain, resentment, guilt, shame, and other emotions I couldn't even put into words without the help of Dr. Bellet. When I left therapy, I literally felt like a new person, again so cliché but true. I was deeply grateful for what God had done for me. And I knew my story wasn't over yet, which filled me with great excitement. I felt very called to marriage and was excited to meet my future husband.

And as God's sense of humor would have it, I had already met him.

CHAPTER 15

Dating Michael

I used to be petrified at the thought of spending the rest of my life with someone, almost to the point of having a panic attack. *After all, who in their right mind would choose me with all of my issues?* I was abused as a child, had an eating disorder in high school and college, struggled with depression, anxiety, suicidal thoughts, daddy issues, had a borderline personality disorder and chronic post-traumatic stress disorder. How's that for *easygoing?*

I pursued men in college because I desperately yearned for attention and affirmation, which only left me feeling more alone and emptier than before. I desperately wanted someone to choose me. I wanted to be enough for someone. I wanted to be called beautiful. I wanted to live life without fear. I wanted to be wanted.

During therapy, my perspective about relationships and marriage slowly started to shift. As I healed, I started to believe that I wasn't a burden like the voice in my head kept telling me. I had the opportunity to learn from the past and see beauty in my suffering. Instead of seeing myself as a victim, I had to make the choice to see myself as a survivor. I could spend the rest of my life thinking that no one would ever love the real me, or I could see myself as a strong, independent, courageous woman. I chose the latter and continue to make that choice today.

The first time I met with Dr. Bellet, he asked why I had called him and why I made the choice to come see him. I looked at him with tears in my eyes and tremendous fear in my voice and said, "I don't want a marriage like my parents. And I don't want to turn out like my dad. I don't want to do to my children what he did to me. I want them to feel loved by me. I want them to be secure in their identity as a son or daughter of God. I don't want them to have to struggle the way I have."

He affirmed my pain, then softly smiled and replied, "I can't guarantee what your future is going to be. But I can guarantee that I will give you the tools you need here in therapy to not let that happen." For the first time in a long time, I was filled with immense hope about marriage and children. I felt like I could do it.

As I was driving to San Diego on September 5, 2013, the feast day of Saint Teresa of Kolkata, I got a call from Michael Preszler. "Hey Maura, this is Michael Preszler. I don't know if you remember me, but we met a few years ago when we talked about the possibility of me doing some film work for Made in His Image. I promise I wasn't stalking you, but I happened to see on Facebook that you are moving to San Diego. I am moving there, too, and I'd love to see you."

I remembered who Michael was, but I was a little surprised to hear from him. We hadn't communicated since New York City. At the same time I was excited to connect with someone in San Diego that I had met before and looked forward to spending time together. Michael and I both moved to San Diego within five days of each other, which was beautifully orchestrated by God. It's no coincidence that Michael called me on Mother Teresa's feast day either, because we had both been on the same life-changing FOCUS mission trip to India, a year apart. God's plans are so incredibly beautiful!

I absolutely loved San Diego! I loved my roommate Kristin, my job, the weather, and making new friends. Michael and

I started spending a lot of time together in groups and one-on-one. We went to a Zac Brown Band concert outside within the first few weeks of being in California. After the concert he walked me to my car and gave me a loaf of pumpkin bread he had made. *Who is this guy?* I wondered. I was usually the one to bake things for people, and it was really nice to have someone bake something for me. I went home and tried the bread, which to this day was the best pumpkin bread I have ever had. Michael and I had so much fun together, and as the weeks passed, I started to develop strong feelings for him.

It was on my heart to tell him that we probably shouldn't spend any more time together one-on-one. That same day Michael called me to tell me he really enjoyed spending time with me and was really attached to me. My heart fluttered. He also said he wasn't ready to date yet and that we should not get together one-on-one anymore. I was disappointed, but I respected him for telling me how he felt.

Three weeks later I heard from a friend that he had taken a girl on date. That night he called me. I was hurt, didn't answer, and threw my phone on my bed. A few hours later he called again, and I answered. He told me he was set up on a blind date and that the whole time he was on the date, he wished he was with me. "I just couldn't stop seeing your beautiful big blue eyes and hearing your laugh. Can I take you on a date this Saturday?"

"I thought you weren't sure of your vocation," I responded.

"I really feel called to date you," he said.

We did start dating again, and it was magical. I felt so alive and carefree with Michael. He was the greatest boyfriend. His attention to detail blew me away. He always planned incredible dates, and I loved spending time with him.

He brought me flowers and wrote me notes. We played games, cooked, baked, and made fancy cocktail drinks, went running and hiking, spent time at the beach, prayed, and went to Mass together. I had prayed for someone like Michael for what seemed like an eternity. One night we were going for a walk, and Michael leaned over and asked if he could hold my hand. At that moment I knew I was going to marry him. For years I had been praying and only ever told God that the man I would marry would ask to hold my hand the first time. Michael was the only man I dated to ever do that.

Five months later, however, Michael broke up with me because he still had doubts about his vocation. He flew back to New York City and spent time with the CFRs there. I was devastated. I handled the breakup really immaturely at times and called and texted him when I knew I shouldn't. He was always so sweet, and I knew I was only hurting myself.

On July 4, 2014, I sat with Michael on the beach in San Diego to watch the fireworks. He had returned from New York, and we needed to talk. I had just returned from Africa and earlier that evening, I had gone for a run along the ocean. I stopped halfway and started crying because I was still so deeply hurt and saddened by the breakup. In between my tears, I heard God the Father say, "I haven't forgotten you, Maura, and I have a plan for you. Trust Me."

Exactly one year later, Michael and I were married. God the Father is a faithful Father.

CHAPTER 16

Letting Go

In 2014 I was working part-time as a pastry chef at Whole Foods and had taken several extra shifts to make some extra money. I called Dr. Bellet and booked a week of therapy, bought a plane ticket, rented a hotel room and car, and flew to Nashville. My time with Dr. Bellet that week was so helpful. I made a little retreat out of the week, and it was really healing. I was hurt that Michael didn't figure out his vocation before we started dating. Dr. Bellet reminded me that if it was meant to be, Michael would come back. He encouraged me to cut off all communication with Michael. I knew in my heart I had to do that, but it was so hard. Dr. Bellet reminded me not to chase Michael. "Men like the thrill of the chase," he told me. "If you chase Michael, he won't be able to chase you." His words struck my heart, and I knew he was right. He also told me that if Michael did come back, I shouldn't run right back to him.

I flew back to California and did exactly what Dr. Bellet said. Several months later Michael called me. "Hi, Maura, how are you? Would you like to go pumpkin picking with me and make a pie together?"

"Is this a date?"

"Yes, it's a date. I want to take you on a date."

I smiled. Even though I was really happy, I was also nervous. I had started moving on, and I didn't want to be hurt again. We got back together in October 2014.

On January 1, 2015, we got engaged in the chapel at Seton Hall University in New Jersey, where I prayed most of my holy hours after returning from India. First Michael gave me a large framed picture of Rembrandt's *The Return of the Prodigal Son*. I literally fell to my knees in tears. That painting held such a special place in my heart and symbolized so much of my recovery. Michael hugged me and told me to stand up. I did, and he proposed. It was one of the most beautiful days of my life.

We flew back to California and started to plan our wedding. In February 2015 my mom filed for a restraining order against my dad because of his violence. I flew to New Jersey for the court case to testify. As I waited anxiously in the witness room, I thought I was going to throw up. When my name was called, I walked into the courtroom, took the stand, and was sworn in. The judge asked me about my childhood. Right there on that stand, I told him the truth. I told him about the abuse and violence, and I told him that my dad had the power to kill my mom and that I was scared for her life.

My dad didn't have an attorney present, and so he cross-examined me. He must have searched the internet for articles I had written associated with Made in His Image along with many interviews I had done. He tried to use the information he had gathered to get my testimony repudiated. He kept saying that because I had suffered from depression and a borderline personality disorder, I wasn't reputable.

The judge asked him if he was a psychologist.

"No, I am not."

The judge then asked if he had a psychologist to represent him.

"No, I do not."

"Then I will allow her testimony." When the judge said those words, I felt so powerful. I locked eyes with my dad and said, "Yes, I have struggled with depression and a borderline personality disorder. I've struggled greatly, and with the help of therapy and medication, I am living in recovery. And for the record, 95 percent of people that struggle with a borderline personality disorder are victims of abuse—abuse that you caused in my case."

My mom was granted the restraining order, and I stayed in New Jersey to visit with her for a week.

On July 4, 2015, Michael and I got married in Bismarck, North Dakota, where his parents live. My brother Matthew walked me down the aisle. Our wedding day was such a holy, exquisite, and magical day, and we both felt God's grace in such a profound way. Our wedding night was immensely pure, beautiful, and without fear, which is something I prayed for specifically.

Marriage has been so healing for me, and Michael is one of the greatest gifts God the Father has blessed me with. Michael always tries to see the good in every situation. He is very humble and knows that anything good he does comes from the Lord, and he truly walks in His confidence. Michael inspires me to continue to live in gratitude. He is such a hard worker and is always so willing to help me with anything I need. He continually sacrifices for me and for our boys. He is always trying to make me feel special and desired. He treats me to special drinks or desserts, oftentimes denying himself to pay for it. He encourages me, surprises me, and in our five-plus years of marriage, I have never heard him complain about anything I have made for dinner or packed him for lunch. He does the dishes and the laundry. But even more than material things, he supports me in my journey of recovery. He is very forgiving and has helped me face immense fears in life by his gentle and affirming spirit and touch. He makes me feel so safe and protected and I am so blessed to be his wife. But most importantly, Michael points me to God the Father daily.

Choosing to See Beauty

CHAPTER 17

Crushing Depression

As I've mentioned, my favorite saint is Saint Padre Pio. Saint Pio is one of the most beloved, astounding, and controversial religious figures of the twentieth century. He bore the wounds of Jesus on his own body, healed the sick, predicted future events, read the minds and consciences of those he counseled, and in some instances appeared miles away to help souls in need. But those who came to see him were less moved by these wonders than by his compassion, warmth, holiness, and profound love for Jesus. In his lifetime he was unjustly accused of neurosis, hysteria, and immorality, but in time he was vindicated, and thirty-four years after his death in 1968, he was named a saint of the Roman Catholic Church.

Francesco Forgione was born in 1887, in the village of Pietrelcina in the south of Italy. He was the second of five children. His parents were poor farmers. An exceedingly pious boy, Francesco had frequent visions of Jesus, Mary, and his guardian angel. At the age of ten, he announced his intention of becoming a Franciscan friar, and he entered the Capuchin novitiate in Morcone at the age of sixteen.

His piety intensified in his late teens and early twenties, and with it his mystical experiences. Jesus appeared and spoke to him, but Satan also assailed Padre Pio with frightening visions, numerous temptations, and even physical assaults. In September 1918, Padre Pio had a vision in the friary chapel. The crucifix transformed into a vision of Jesus crucified, and from this vision came rays of light that pierced his hands and feet. Within a year enormous crowds began coming to San Giovanni, and Padre Pio spent sixteen hours a day in the confessional.

St. Pio endured extraordinary persecution from jealous clergy. From 1931–1933, he was forbidden to hear confessions or say Mass in public. During this period Padre Pio appeared cheerful but was equally well-known for outbursts of temper toward curious pilgrims and unrepentant sinners. He underwent continual darkness and doubt whether he was in a state of grace. He never thought of himself as "holy."

After World War II ended, Padre Pio embarked on a new mission—to build a hospital in the community. He began organizing a board of directors in 1946. Donations poured in from admirers and disciples around the world, and in 1956 the House for the Relief of Suffering opened its doors. It is known today as a world-class medical institution. On September 23, 1968, fifty years after receiving the stigmata, Padre Pio died. He was beatified in 1999 and canonized in 2002 by Saint John Paul II. Over eight million people visit his tomb each year.

A few days before Christmas 2016, I was getting a pedicure while holding my eight-month-old son, Pio. I was thinking about all I had to do that evening when the lady sitting next to me answered her phone. Her voice was somber as she spoke. "Yeah, I've had a really difficult week. My nephew took his life on Tuesday, and my brother and his wife are really struggling. He had struggled with depression for ten years and now it's over."

I held my son close, kissed him, and tried to fight back tears. My heart ached for this woman and her nephew's parents. I can't even fathom the immense pain of losing a child. I drove home, put my son down for his nap, and cried.

There is so much beauty in the world, and Christmas is a special time, but it's also coupled with tremendous suffering and pain. Yes, it's Christmas, but that doesn't mean you need to smile all day and put on an act if you are struggling. It's okay to not be okay. I learned this in a tangible way while pregnant with Pio.

Three weeks after our wedding, I found out I was pregnant with Pio. Michael and I were both ecstatic. I called my psychiatrist the next day to make an appointment because I knew the medication I was on wasn't recommended for pregnant mothers. The following week, I saw her and we worked out a plan to taper off my medication within eight days. For months afterward I suffered from withdrawal symptoms that at times left me unable to drive.

The days turned to weeks and the weeks to months, and I felt like life was being sucked out of me, even though I was carrying this precious new life. Each day I sunk deeper into immense darkness and a total lack of feeling. It was such a dark and lonely time, even though my husband couldn't have been more compassionate and encouraging. I seriously don't think I would have survived without him. I was exceedingly nauseous and most days I would literally put a towel on the bathroom floor and just hang my head over the toilet. Other pregnant mothers told me they were nauseous during their pregnancies, too, and I felt like they handled it way better than I did. I seriously wondered what the heck was wrong with me. I also felt so guilty because Michael and I were so newly married and I wanted this to be a carefree and fun time. Even though he continued to reassure me that he was there for me and that everything was going to be okay, I felt so much shame.

When people found out I was pregnant, they would comment, "Oh you're pregnant—what a beautiful time, so full of life. Isn't it just the best?" I would fake a smile and nod and think to myself, *No this is not the best, and I feel miserable.* I felt like a horrible mother, plagued with guilt and shame. *Why wasn't I happy? What was wrong with me? Why couldn't I feel anything?*

I was ashamed of how I felt. After all, isn't a woman supposed to just love everything about pregnancy and be thankful for the new life within her? Isn't she supposed to just glow with happiness? What happens if you don't glow? Because I never got the glow. Trust me, I waited for it, but it never came. Just more nausea and vomiting. And there was nothing glowing about that.

I was terrified that my baby would feel unwanted and unloved. I cried out to God to help me but nothing came. I found a cozy little Saint Padre Pio chapel that was close to our home where I could go to pray. I begged Jesus to help me through Saint Pio's intercession. We were going to name our son Francis or William, and we didn't decide on Pio until after he was born. Looking back, I see that Padre Pio was interceding for all three of us.

In December 2015, my low plummeted even lower and the thoughts of suicide I struggled with in college returned. I was petrified. I didn't want these thoughts, and I definitely didn't want to die. I just wanted to be a *normal* pregnant first-time mom and enjoy time with Michael. We had plans to fly to Michael's family for Christmas in North Dakota, and I sincerely wondered how I was going to do it. When Michael came home from work the evening before we were scheduled to leave, I was sobbing when he opened the door. I told him I couldn't do it. I couldn't leave at 3:00 a.m. to drive four hours to the airport, I couldn't pack, I couldn't be around a crowd of people, and I couldn't fake anymore smiles and pretend everything was okay when I could barely shower and brush my teeth. I felt like a horrible wife, daughter-in-law and mother and my son wasn't even born yet. *How could I take care of him once he got here? How was I going to take care of a newborn when I couldn't even take care of myself?* I loathed myself for keeping Michael from his siblings and parents. And to make matters worse, we couldn't get a refund for the tickets. Michael kept reassuring me not to worry about the money and told me he just wanted to help me and sit with me in my pain.

That night thoughts of suicide kept racing through my mind. I didn't welcome the thoughts, I didn't have a plan, and I didn't act on them, but they were there nonetheless, and I couldn't get them out of my head. The pain was suffocating me, and I could feel myself sinking into despair. Michael held me on the bathroom floor as I clutched my Rosary beads. There was no doubt in my mind, my depression was back and I didn't know how I was going to make it through the rest of the pregnancy.

I slept from 12:00 to 2:00 a.m. in Michael's arms, and we both woke up at the same time. We talked and I told him we should go to North Dakota. I could tell he was extremely hesitant. We ended up going, and it was one of the hardest Christmases I've ever experienced. I had to mentally get myself through each minute. I had no joy and really no feeling at all. I was numb. On Christmas day I snuck into an empty room and just wept alone. Michael found me, and we cried together. I was convinced I was a bad mother already. I thought our son would be better off with another mother. Michael gently reminded me that God's plan was the best plan for our son. I didn't want to waste my suffering and tried my best to offer it for our son, for his sanctity, vocation, purity, and faith.

In my deepest and darkest moments of depression, I tried to remember the following which is one of my favorite quotes. I know I did it very imperfectly but I think God looks at our desire and not perfection.

> *Every tear, disappointment and grieved heart*
> *is a blank check. If we write our name on it, it is*
> *worthless. If we sign it with Christ's name, it is*
> *infinite in its value. In prosperity, Christ gives you*
> *His gifts; in suffering with faith, he gives you Himself.*

Fulton Sheen

We returned from our trip, and after seeing my doctor, I was immediately placed back on my medication. Again I felt guilty. *What if it caused our son to have a birth defect?* Michael reminded me again that we had to trust God, and the doctor reminded me that I needed to be healthy to bring Pio into the world.

It wasn't an immediate fix, and I worried immensely that I would suffer from postpartum depression. Our son was born on April 17, 2016, at 2:43 a.m. after twenty-two hours of labor and two hours of pushing. During labor I was just so thankful that God had brought me to this day safely. The moment I saw Pio's face, I knew it had all been worth it. The doctor placed Pio on my chest, and he curled up and fell asleep as I held him. It's a moment I'll never forget. I have goosebumps as I write this because it was so profound meeting Pio. I whispered to him, *You are so loved, little one, and I'd do it all again to just see your face. I love you so much it hurts.*

Pio was born completely healthy and was such a joyful and happy baby. My husband and I are so thankful for the gift that he is to us. I haven't struggled with depression since my pregnancy with Pio, and I am so thankful to God for the gift of a healthy body and mind.

Four-and-a-half months after Pio was born, I went to a Catholic doctor in Fallbrook, California. Michael and I were practicing Natural Family Planning (NFP), and I really wanted to see a Catholic OBGYN. The nurse did some tests, and then Dr. Stigen came in, looked me in the eyes, and said, "You're pregnant." I fought so hard to hold back the tears that formed in my eyes. She gently touched my hand and said, "It's okay to cry." Her permission unleashed a torrent of emotions within me, one of them being guilt.

I did not know how I could take care of Pio and go through another pregnancy so soon. I was consumed with fear. My second pregnancy turned out to be fairly easy, though, and my fear of having two children so close in age lessened over time.

Noah was born on June 15, 2017, after ten hours of labor and twenty-five minutes of pushing. Michael and I thank God and praise Him for the greatest surprise we didn't know our hearts and family needed. Noah is the sweetest little guy, so full of life and joy. He was born with a severe gross motor delay, and to see him work so hard during the first three years of his life in physical and occupational therapy was amazing to witness. Noah has taught me to much about hard work and determination. The first time he pulled himself up in the pool to climb out, I was overjoyed for him. He smiled and came running to me, saying, "I did it, Mama. I did it." I hugged him so tightly. I'm beyond blessed to be his mother and couldn't even begin to imagine life without our sweet Noah.

Sometimes it can be really difficult to remember that God is in control. It's scary to let go and let Him take over. Noah is such a witness to God's goodness and beauty. Whatever you are going through, remember that God is near. He will not abandon you. You are never alone. Trust that the Creator of all things knows what you need. He holds you in the palm of His hand.

CHAPTER 18

The Beauty of Motherhood

I love being a mother, and it's so beautiful to see Michael as the father of our children. He is an incredible, playful, affirming, and patient dad. Motherhood has also been very healing, and one of those moments happened on Easter Sunday in 2019.

On Holy Saturday I went to Target to get some Easter treats for Pio and Noah. It brought me so much joy to pick out little gifts for their Easter baskets. I love to see them smile, and I looked forward to Easter morning. There is a tremendous amount of sibling rivalry between them, so I made sure to pick out the same gifts for each to them to eliminate any fighting over Easter toys and candy. At the time Pio had just turned three and Noah was twenty-two months.

Michael and I loved seeing their faces on Easter morning when they saw their baskets. Pio had been asking for his Easter basket for most of Lent, and I kept reminding him that he could have it on Easter morning when Jesus rose from the dead. I would read him a children's story about Easter to help him understand. In his little mind this translated to Jesus coming out of a tunnel like one of his trains. Even though their Easter baskets, toys, and treats were identical, it was funny to see Pio lean over to make sure Noah didn't have anything he didn't have in his basket.

We went to Easter morning Mass and then to a friend's house for brunch and an Easter egg hunt. After the Easter egg hunt, we went home to take a nap before going to our friends Carrie and Leo's house for dinner. It was a beautiful day.

That night as Michael and I were saying prayers before drifting off to sleep, he asked me what I was grateful for. I was exhausted and thought I would fall asleep before we finished prayers, but that night was different. Soft tears rolled down my cheeks as I said, "I'm thankful Pio and Noah will never have anxiety over an Easter egg hunt or wonder if you are going to hide their Easter eggs." Michael held me close and whispered, "Me too."

One of my biggest triggers and fears growing up as a little girl was Easter. I had tremendous anxiety during the weeks and days leading up to Easter. There was a neighborhood Easter egg hunt on Holy Saturday, and I never knew if my dad was going to hide my siblings and my Easter eggs or not. If my mom and dad were fighting, he would take his anger out on us by threatening not to hide our eggs. To a sensitive little girl, this was so harmful and damaging. I never understood why he made us pray from 12:00 to 3:00 p.m. on Good Friday but would then treat us so dysfunctionally. I remember feeling sick to my stomach and not being able to eat because I was so nervous about the Easter eggs.

It filled me with copious amounts of joy to watch Pio and Noah run around trying to find their Easter eggs. They were so carefree and free from fear, as a child on Easter should be, and it flooded my heart with immense gratitude. I know with certainty that they will never feel anxiety over whether their dad is going to hide their Easter eggs or not. I'm so thankful they will never have to know that pain.

I know as a mother that I can't protect them from all pain in their lives. They are going to experience pain and loss in their lives at some point. But I'm so happy it won't be over something as innocent as an Easter egg hunt. I'm so grateful to God for redeeming such a painful memory, as only He can. He truly does make all things new. Easter is such a special redemption song for my heart.

Michael and I both have a strong desire to teach our children about their emotions and feelings and know the importance of recognizing them. We teach the boys that it's okay for them to express their feelings. It's okay to be sad. It's okay to cry and be hurt.

Early one Sunday morning in July 2019, our family drove to the airport to drop off Michael and Noah. Pio and I were going to follow them in two days to Bismarck, North Dakota, to visit Michael's family. I knew that Pio would be really upset when we dropped off Michael and Noah because he would want to go too. I thought about bringing a lollipop in the car so that I could give it to Pio when he had a meltdown as he watched them leave. But we decided that it would be best for Pio if we allowed him to feel sad because if we just handed him a lollipop when he cried, he wouldn't learn how to acknowledge his feelings, but instead might just suppress or dismiss them. We want to raise emotionally intelligent children.

You wouldn't just hand a friend in distress a bowl of ice cream, would you? A good friend would sit with that distressed friend and listen to them. Someone in pain wants to be heard and seen. And this is what we want to teach our children.

Pio was very upset when we left the airport, but it turned out to be a beautiful, teachable moment. I tried to reassure him that I understood he was upset and wanted to go with Daddy and Noah to Grandma and Grandpa's house. I told him it was okay to be sad. I told him I was there for him and reassured him that we would be going soon. I let him talk, and I listened. When we returned from the airport, I held him on the couch. "Pio sad," he said. It was hard to watch him struggle and be sad, but it was also beautiful to hear him name his feelings and emotions, which is so important. Because if we don't name it, we can't allow ourselves to fully feel something.

As a society, I feel like showing our emotions is seen as a sign of weakness, but this simply isn't true. When we share our weakness, we make ourselves vulnerable, and when we make ourselves vulnerable, we show our strength.

> *I knew that the only thing I could do was to be with you, stay with you and somehow encourage you not to run away from your pain, but to trust that you had the strength to stand in it. Now, many years later, you can say that, indeed, you could stand in your pain and grow strong through it. At the moment, it seemed an impossible task, and, still, it was the only task to which I could call you.*

> *My own experience with anguish has been that facing it and living it through, is the way to healing. But I cannot do that on my own. I need someone to keep me standing in it, to assure me that there is peace beyond the anguish, life beyond death and love beyond fear. But I know now, at least, that attempting to avoid, repress or escape the pain is like cutting off a limb that could be healed with proper attention.*

> Henri Nouwen, *Life of the Beloved*

Appendix

PRACTICAL ADVICE ON ABUSE RECOVERY AND A LOVED ONE'S SEXUAL ADDICTION

If you are recovering from abuse or a loved one's sexual addiction, I am so very sorry for your pain. I would like to offer you some practical advice that helped me in my journey of healing.

Allow yourself to be angry and to truly feel the frustration you experience. This is a natural part of the healing process, and if you don't permit yourself to get upset, it will only surface later. Don't internalize the pain; Jesus Himself wept when He was sorrowful.

Talk to a psychologist who believes in the evils of pornography. Don't let yourself believe the lie that if you go to therapy or talk about your feelings, you are weak. On the contrary, it signifies your courageous spirit and the fact that you desire to deal with an issue that needs to be dealt with. I promise you, if you suppress your feelings and emotions, they will surface again. Jesus longs for you to be whole in body, mind, and spirit. There is absolutely nothing wrong with talking to a psychologist. I truly believe that mental health professionals are instruments of Jesus' healing.

I also encourage you to get to know God as your Father. I highly recommend the book, *The Return of the Prodigal Son* by Henri Nouwen. Spend time in front of the Blessed Sacrament listening and talking to God. Talk to Him throughout the day and tell Him how much it hurts.

Ask Him to protect you, ask Him to show you who you are as His daughter, and tell Him you want to see beauty in yourself. Then let Him love you. This is often a challenge when you have been deeply wounded, but our Father's love is safe, and He longs to protect you.

A very obvious question that arises and one that I asked countless times is, *If He desires to protect me, then why did He allow this to happen? If He is such a good God then why would He allow evil to happen?* We are human, and this question appeals particularly to our humanity and is a good question to ask. But we are not God, and we lack the depth and understanding that He possesses. It's important to remember that people are given free will and can therefore do good or evil with it. When abuse and sexual sin happens, it's because people are misusing their free will. This was key for me to keep in mind.

We may never know until eternity why God has allowed certain things to happen. While it's only natural to ask questions, remember that the Cross is the crowning jewel of our faith. You must believe that, and if you don't, then ask for the grace to want to believe it. It's important to also surround yourself with positivity and community. We are not meant to live the Christian faith alone. We need other people, especially when we are going through a difficult time.

Look in the mirror daily, without any makeup on, and say, "I'm beautiful because I'm a daughter of God. And He doesn't create ugly." Even if you don't *feel* like saying it, say it. It takes an extreme act of the will to overcome negative thoughts that consume us.

I encourage you to write out a battle plan for your healing and be vigilant about following through with it, especially when moments of doubt and fear strike you. You mustn't wallow in your pain, but you can't rush your healing either. Give yourself grace and ask a psychologist to help you achieve a balance between the two.

When I was diagnosed with post-traumatic stress disorder from the doctors at the Institute for the Psychological Sciences, one of them told me she could compare me to a soldier returning from war. So I wrote out a battle plan just like soldiers have when they are overseas. I followed the battle plan I made in front of the Blessed Sacrament every day. Yes, there were days I didn't *feel* like going to Mass, praying, taking my medicine, going to therapy, eating well, and exercising, but I did those things anyway. I truly believe I am alive today because of the grace from daily Communion and my time in front of our Creator and Lord. During my darkest moments, He never let go of me; He only held me tighter.

Pray for the person who hurt you, but not excessively. You can't *save* them, and it's important to remember that. A priest once told me, "To forgive is to mirror the Divine," and this is what we are called to do. We are called to demonstrate the Father's love to those who have wounded us. I'm not saying it's easy, because it's not. Jesus Himself gave us an example to follow when He hung from the Cross on Calvary to redeem us. He prayed, "Father, forgive them, for they know not what they do."

It's vital to frequent the sacraments as often as possible. If you think you don't have time, then make the time. Get up an hour early, find a noon Mass you can go to on your lunch break, or find a chapel that has Adoration in the evenings. Again, when you don't *feel* like going, go anyway. The graces available to you through the Holy Sacrifice of the Mass are incalculable. Jesus yearns to give Himself to you; He thirsts to be your Savior and Healer.

I encourage you to watch one of my favorite movies, *The Human Experience*. The documentary seeks to discover the meaning of life and aims to answer questions such as *Who am I? Why am I here? Where am I going? What is my purpose in life?*

The main actor, Jeffrey Azize, touched my heart. Several times during the movie, he talks about his childhood and how he seeks to forgive and show mercy to those who have hurt him, mainly his father. There are two scenes that moved me to tears. In one he is being filmed in a taxi in New York City, and as he gazes out the window, he talks about how challenging it was to feel and experience love when the ones who were supposed to love and care for him fell from grace and harmed him. It was exceedingly profound! I wept during that part because I could so relate to his words.

In another scene he meets his father after years of separation, and he embraces him. To love those who have harmed us is to reflect the Father's love, and this is our mission in life.

PRACTICAL ADVICE ON THE FATHER WOUND AND MENTAL HEALTH

I truly believe one of the most pandemic wounds in our world is fatherlessness. Every little girl yearns to be cherished by her father. She desires to be wanted. She asks: "Do you delight in me? Am I worth fighting for? Do you want me? Do you see me? Do you value me? Am I beautiful? Am I enough?" When these questions are answered through a father appropriately loving, touching, kissing, and affirming his daughter, she doesn't need to fill that void in her heart with fleeting pleasures. She is firmly rooted in her identity.

But when these questions aren't answered in an appropriate way, she seeks to find these answers on her own. When a father doesn't give his daughter the attention and love she craves, her need for male acceptance is bottomless. Oftentimes these unanswered questions lead to eating disorders, depression, and promiscuity. Please note: these struggles can still be present with a loving father, but the likelihood is exponentially higher without one.

All of my life I've yearned for love. I craved physical touch so deeply at times that I thought I'd explode without it. I've ached for it, yet I've feared it with every fiber of my being. I was abused so much I didn't even know what good physical touch should feel like. As a little girl and teenager, I was never told I was beautiful or enough. These unanswered questions left my curiosity with a hunger that couldn't satisfy my heart. I searched for these answers on my own. I thought if I achieved a certain weight, I would feel beautiful and enough. But the truth is, the more weight I lost, the emptier I felt.

Before I went to therapy, practically every time I saw a little girl and her father, I would tear up or begin crying hysterically. In therapy I learned I had to grieve that loss. My heart yearned for a father who loved me, for a father who protected me, for a father who told me I was beautiful, for a father who loved my mother. Before therapy, I thought those thoughts weren't valid.

I don't need a dad, I would tell myself. *I'm strong. I can take care of myself.* In therapy I learned that my desires for a father were good, for this is the way God created my heart. This is the way He creates every little girl's heart. This is a desire that He Himself has placed in us. This is a good desire, and it is important to acknowledge that.

Grieving the loss of the dad I wanted was vital. You can't move on if you don't first acknowledge the pain and allow yourself to feel the weight of what was lost. Sometimes I still wish I had a different dad, but those thoughts are rare now. And when they do come to mind, I have the tools to deal with the pain from my time in therapy. I acknowledge the thoughts, say a quick prayer, and do my best to live in gratitude for what I do have.

I used to be ashamed of my story. There was so much pain that I couldn't navigate and make sense of. Then I discovered God as my Father, I went to therapy, took medication, and did the hard work. It wasn't easy, but I am so grateful for my journey. I certainly haven't arrived. No one has, for life is a journey home to Heaven. I will keep learning, growing, and healing. I will keep forgiving, loving, and showing up. I never dreamed that God would use my story the way He has. I'm humbled. I'm thankful to be a wounded healer.

PRACTICAL ADVICE ON MENTAL HEALTH

Depression and anxiety are not the result of failing to pray enough. Unfortunately, many Catholics make the mistake of thinking you can pray your way out of a mental illness, which is dangerous thinking. There is so much shame and guilt covering mental illnesses that many people are afraid to reach out and ask for help.

Yes, Jesus could cure you at any time, and we need to have faith, but we also need to utilize modern healthcare and medicine. If you were diagnosed with cancer, would you just go to church and pray? No, you would go to the doctors. You would talk about it. You would follow the treatment plan your doctors gave you. Why would you not do the same with a mental illness? More people die of suicide related to a mental illness than they do from cancer. We need both Jesus and psychology.

Depression, anxiety, eating disorders, addictions, bipolar disorder, borderline personality disorder, and other mental illnesses should not be taken lightly. God has a plan for you in your pain, and it's also important for you to take action in your recovery.

I've seen mental illnesses take the lives of many people, and it's very sad that even today they are sometimes not viewed as seriously as they should be. It's my sincere hope that if you are struggling and need therapy and medication, you don't feel shame for pursuing those healthy options. I hope you feel brave, because that is truly what you are.

When I struggled with suicidal thoughts in college, people would say things like "Just think happy thoughts or try to do something nice for yourself."

I remember thinking, *You have no clue what this is like. You have no idea what it's like to see your own bottle of prescription drugs and want to swallow the whole thing. Or how it feels to want to jump off every bridge you see, drown yourself in the pool, smash your car into the median on the highway, or pray that you just don't wake up in the morning.*

Then morning comes, and you can't get out of bed. Brushing your hair becomes an accomplishment, washing a load of laundry earns you at least a four-hour nap because it was that exhausting, and getting out of the house feels like running a marathon.

The darkness feels like it's going to suffocate you. You can't think about tomorrow or next week because that's too overwhelming. You can't even think five minutes from the present moment; thirty seconds is enough. The pain is relentless. You feel like you're in a dark hole, and you can't seem to find the light. You want to get out, but you don't know how. You are always tired, even after sleeping for fourteen hours, and you can't stop crying. It's a bleak, lonely, and scary place to be. One thing that keeps a person alive in these situations is hope.

If this season of life is hard for you, I want you to know that you are seen, heard, and loved. I'm so sorry for your pain. I know it hurts, but please stay. Stay because you deserve recovery. Stay to be loved. Stay because you are worthy of love. Stay because our loving Father sent His only Son into the world to die for you. That is how much you are loved.

When I was in therapy and my doctor told me that he was proud of me for the progress I was making, at the time I couldn't see the progress I was making and went home to ask a roommate what she thought. I'll never forget her words of encouragement to me and how she listed things she could vividly see in areas I was improving in. Sometimes it's hard to see our own progress.

When setbacks happen—and they will—they can be very disappointing. It can be tempting to think you haven't progressed at all when this really isn't the case. Setbacks are simply part of the journey and will make you stronger if you let them.

Therapy taught me that healing isn't a straight line. It's important to remember this because our healing is such an ongoing journey. But with God, therapy, medication, rest, friends, loved ones, exercise, and prayer, we have the tools to succeed. We have the tools to be victorious against our demons.

Please remember that it's okay to take a break. It's okay to take medication. It's okay to go to therapy. It's okay to talk about your feelings. It's okay to reach out for help. It's okay to accept help. It's okay to admit you aren't okay. It's okay to rest. It's okay to reach out when things aren't going well. It's okay to ask your friends to support you when you're struggling.

When you call a therapist to set up an appointment, you are brave. When you go to your first therapy appointment, you are brave. When you reach out for help, you are brave. When you admit you're not okay, you are brave. When you go on a first date, you are brave. When you say goodbye to someone who you thought was your forever, you are brave. When you stand up for yourself, you are brave. When you look in the mirror and say, "I'm beautiful," you are brave. When you go a day without weighing yourself, you are brave. When you work out to strengthen your body, you are brave. When you call a friend to check in, you are brave. When you share your story, you are brave. When you discover that not everyone will hurt you, you are brave. When you believe that you are lovable, you are brave.

You are not a burden. Reaching out and asking for help doesn't make you selfish. It makes you brave.

PRACTICAL ADVICE ON RELATIONSHIPS

When things aren't going our way, it can be so easy to think that God has forgotten about us and that He has a plan for everyone but us. In these moments of fear and doubt, it's important to fill our minds with truth. And the truth is, God does have a plan for you, and His love story for you is a million times better than the best one you could write for yourself.

If you are doubting God's plan for your life, going through a breakup, feeling alone, rejected, and abandoned, please remember that God can't be outdone in generosity. He desires to bless you and grant the desires of your heart.

If you long for marriage and this is God's will for you, He will bring your spouse into your life when the time is right. Your job right now is to discover what God wants to teach you during this season of waiting. I know it may feel as if everyone around you is in a relationship, getting married, and having babies, and you are wondering when your time will come. I promise you that what God has in store for you is worth the wait.

God will never show you gold and give you silver. He desires to grant the longings of your heart, even though it feels like He is taking forever. One day you will look back at this time of waiting and see how He was preparing you for your vocation.

Share your heart and feelings with God today; he is waiting to listen to you. Let Him surprise you with a love more beautiful than you can imagine. And be gentle with yourself so you can learn what He wants to teach you through the process. And remember, until Jesus is enough for you, I promise you that no man will ever be.

If God created a woman for Adam when he was the only man on earth, take comfort in knowing He hasn't forgotten your love story. If He is calling you to marriage, He has someone handpicked just for you.

Date the man who leads you closer to Jesus instead of to his bed. Date the man who thinks you're beautiful without your hair and makeup done because trust me, you won't always have your hair and makeup done once you're married.

Marry the man who will lead you to Heaven, who will join your sufferings to his, and journey with you to becoming the best you can be.

It takes courage to love and let yourself be loved, but nothing good is ever achieved without vulnerability. Don't lower your standards to find him, because if you do, it won't be love that you find. You are worth being pursued, cherished, and protected. Don't settle for less.

Interpersonal relationships are often very difficult for survivors of abuse. Dating and marrying Michael was a tremendous feat for me. We have only been married for five years, and it's incredible to see how I have grown during this time. While I am definitely not perfect, I am so thankful I went to therapy before getting married to have the tools to know how to communicate, have appropriate conflict, and resolve disagreements maturely.

A few months after we were engaged, we got in a big disagreement. I don't even remember what it was about, but I vividly remember the anxiety I felt because I thought Michael was going to leave.

I turned my phone off and went for a run to clear my head. When I got back to my apartment, Michael was standing on my front porch with flowers and coffee. Even though the conflict wasn't resolved that day, I remember him telling me before he left my apartment to go home that he wasn't going anywhere and that he was committed to our relationship.

It took me a long time to find Michael, but he was worth the wait. And I want to encourage you that men like this exist. You are worth a man who will reassure you. You are worth a man who will try to help calm your fears. Don't settle. Please don't settle.

From my relationship with Michael, I have learned that not all men will leave. Michael was and still is very good at reminding me that he isn't looking for reasons to leave me and that he isn't going anywhere. He accepts me and loves me for who I am, with my past, insecurities, and brokenness.

I am worth this and so are you. You are worth the committed heart. You are worth the pursuit. You are worth a man who desires your good. You are worth a man who will journey to Heaven with you. You are worthy of love.

Marriage is a journey to Heaven. I believe so many marriages end in divorce because we have forgotten how to serve one another; we have forgotten how to love. Authentic love is getting up for the fifth time during the night with a crying baby. Authentic love is serving your spouse and being present when you don't want to. Authentic love is speaking kindly, forgiving, and seeing the good in your spouse. Authentic love is changing the tenth dirty diaper for the day, wiping peanut butter faces, and cleaning up an endless amount of crumbs off the flour. Authentic love is showing up. Authentic love is service.

If we are looking to another flawed human to make us happy and fulfill our hearts, we will never find happiness. Happiness is found in laying down your life for something greater than yourself.

Practical Advice on Body Image

After my battle with anorexia, I struggled with binge eating and obsessive exercising. Most days I would go all day without eating and then binge eat at night. I would go to bed so disgusted with myself and full of shame. Each night I promised myself that tomorrow would be different. But it wasn't.

I would exercise obsessively to try and burn the calories from the night before. I had starved myself for so long that when I started eating again, I couldn't stop eating. I tried to plan meals with friends so I could eat a normal dinner, but I always ended up binging late at night. Sometimes I would just skip dinner and go straight to a binge. It was horrible, and the cycle of shame was overwhelming. I didn't know how to admit that I needed help.

When I struggled with anorexia, people noticed that I was getting thinner, but with binge eating no one noticed. I gained over twenty pounds during those years of binge eating. I kept it up for years without a single comment. I feared being exposed but yearned for it at the same time. To put it in perspective for you, I weighed more during my cycles of binge eating than on the days I gave birth to my sweet babies.

In therapy I learned that my struggles with food were born out of my strong need to be in control of something. As I reflect on my childhood, I see that I struggled the most with food when my parents fought the most and the abuse was more regular. I learned that when the control and stability I so desperately sought was slipping from my grasp, I had the tendency to cling even harder to my eating disorder because at least I was in control of that. I do not blame my parents for my struggle with an eating disorder, though; it was simply a relief to understand the psychology behind my struggle.

My three biggest trigger foods were peanut butter, chocolate brownie ice cream, and Fritos. I would consume them in disgusting amounts. It wasn't until I went to therapy that I completely stopped. There is always an underlying cause of an eating disorder. Abuse was mine, and until I talked about it, I couldn't completely stop the horrible cycle.

It's been ten years since the last time I binged and overexercised. I waited two years before I bought peanut butter and chocolate brownie ice cream and ten years before I bought Fritos again.

In the spring of 2019, I bought a bag of Fritos for the first time since binging. I was nervous but mostly thankful. They tasted so good. I was with my husband, and when we got home, he took the bag and divided them into individual portions for me. Instead of being riddled with shame and fear, I was overwhelmed by Michael's support. It was his idea to divide the Fritos into separate bags, but he didn't want to force me. He said he would only do it if I thought it would be helpful. Each day he left one bag for me on the counter with an encouraging note. I remember the days I wanted to binge eat Fritos so badly I could literally taste them. I'm glad God's grace is stronger than the taste of Fritos.

If you are struggling with binge eating, know that there is hope. There will be hard moments, but there is so much joy found in freedom. I encourage you to go to therapy and lean on friends and loved ones. Get accountability and give yourself grace, but most importantly ask God to help you, because He will.

I don't want you to think my struggle with body image just disappeared when I stopped binging. While it lessened significantly, it returned full force when I got pregnant with my first son, Pio. What was different about my struggle, though, as opposed to before therapy was that this time I knew who God the Father is and who I am as His daughter. Knowing this truth changes everything, and while it didn't magically make my struggle disappear, it gave me the tools to combat the lies in my head with God's truth.

I know now that I need to pray every day. I try to start my day with fifteen minutes of silence, and this is vital for me. It is through silence that I have gotten to know God as my Father. Then I spend some time reading the Bible or a devotional book.

I make sure I am moving my body daily because this helps me feel good mentally. I don't scroll through Facebook and Instagram. In my opinion, it's a waste of time. Two years ago for Lent, I took Facebook and Instagram off my phone, and it was one of the best things I've ever done. First, I was spending too much time on social media, and second, it didn't help my struggle with body image. I repeatedly would compare myself to women on social media that had perfectly curated photos, and it wasn't healthy.

It was very hard but liberating to take social media off my phone. I'm not saying social media is bad because there are many positive aspects to it. But if you find that you are spending hours scrolling and comparing yourself to people, many of whom you don't even know, it is probably time for a social media cleanse. Don't worry, it's not going anywhere, and you can always put it back on your phone. Spend your time with your real-life friends; I promise you'll find it freeing when you don't feel the need to document every coffee, ice cream, and outfit purchase.

I don't diet or count calories. Research shows that diets don't work; instead I have made my eating habits a lifestyle choice and now the good habits last. It takes hard work, but it is definitely possible—and there is nothing wrong with having an occasional treat. What I have discovered over my years of hard work with eating and my struggle with body image is that eating is all about balance.

When I shop for clothes, I focus on how the clothes feel while on my body, not the number on the label. One pivotal moment for me was when I bought my wedding dress. I remember going out to lunch with my mother-in-law before we went shopping, and for a moment I felt anxious because I didn't want to eat before shopping. But I took a moment to regroup in my mind, prayed, and reminded myself that I was going to shop for a dress that fit my body. It helped me calm down, and I had the most incredible experience shopping for my wedding dress, full stomach and all.

If you are struggling with loving the body God gave you, I want you to know that there is tremendous hope. There will be hard moments, but there is so much joy found in freedom. If you're struggling, I want to lovingly encourage you to take some time and address the root cause of your struggle. Why do you think you struggle with body image and loving yourself?

Delve into that question—I assure you it will be worth it. Lasting healing happens when we address the underlying cause of a wound. Talk to a counselor, get accountability, lean on friends and loved ones, do the hard work, give yourself grace, and most importantly, ask God to help you in your struggle. Jesus desires to heal you. He desires to help you right here and now in your brokenness. You don't need to be perfect to approach Him, so go to Him now in your pain. Let Him love you through it; I promise, He will. My dear friend, know that freedom awaits you on the other side of vulnerability.

Epilogue

To the girl who stands in front of the mirror criticizing every inch of her body, *you are beautiful. You are valuable. You are enough.*

To the girl who thinks she needs to lose fifteen pounds for a man to ever love her, *you are beautiful. You are valuable. You are enough.*

To the girl who can't keep her dinner down because the number of calories consumes her every thought, *you are beautiful. You are valuable. You are enough.*

To the girl who starves herself all day and binges at night, *you are beautiful. You are valuable. You are enough.*

To the girl who exercises for three hours a day because she is driven to lose weight, *you are beautiful. You are valuable. You are enough.*

To the girl who cries on the cold hard tile of her bathroom floor, bloody razor in hand, *you are beautiful. You are valuable. You are enough.*

To the girl who wears a long sleeve shirt in the middle of July to hide all of her scars, *you are beautiful. You are valuable. You are enough.*

To the girl who gulps down pills just to feel normal for a while, *you are beautiful. You are valuable. You are enough.*

To the girl who stays in bed all day crying because she's too depressed to get up for class, *you are beautiful. You are valuable. You are enough.*

To the girl who thinks she constantly needs to give her body to men for attention, *you are beautiful. You are valuable. You are enough.*

To the girl who reveals her body for all to see, when all she desires is to be seen for the beauty in her heart, *you are beautiful. You are valuable. You are enough.*

To the girl who yearns for physical touch and craves attention and affection, *you are beautiful. You are valuable. You are enough.*

To the girl who drinks more alcohol than water to drown her thoughts and feelings, *you are beautiful. You are valuable. You are enough.*

To the girl who watches the one she loves fall in love with someone else, *you are beautiful. You are valuable. You are enough.*

To the girl whose mother tells her she isn't enough, *you are beautiful. You are valuable. You are enough.*

To the girl whose father beats her, *you are beautiful. You are valuable. You are enough.*

To the girl who locks her bedroom door whenever her dad's been drinking, *you are beautiful. You are valuable. You are enough.*

To the girl who won't go home at night because her parents are always fighting, *you are beautiful. You are valuable. You are enough.*

To the girl who feels hopeless and alone, *you are beautiful. You are valuable. You are enough.*

To the girl who doesn't want to live anymore, *you are beautiful. You are valuable. You are enough.*

I hope you always remember that a bruised and broken heart is actually quite beautiful, because it reveals the tenderness of the human spirit. Don't journey through life thinking you have to be perfect in order to be enough for someone. The truth is, we are all broken.

I love that Jesus chose to rise from the dead on Easter Sunday with scars on His hands, feet and side. He could have appeared flawless, but instead he modeled something beautiful for us. He gave us permission to be authentic, to be real, to be ourselves.

Healing doesn't come from ignoring our wounds or our humanity, but by participating with God as we embrace our wounds and stories. We all have wounds and scars, and this world needs you to embrace yours.

Note from the Publisher

Become who you are.

These words from Pope St. John Paul II have echoed in my heart since I first heard them in 1997 at World Youth Day in Paris. I formed the CatholicPsych Institute to empower people to become who they are by providing services and resources that integrate authentic Catholic anthropology with sound psychological science.

For almost a decade, we have been helping people and organizations develop the skills and knowledge they need to thrive. We develop resources, mentorship, assessment, and psychotherapeutic services to help ecclesial institutions, businesses, families, and individuals reorient themselves to the true nature of who God created them to be. We have now created the CatholicPsych Press to expand the resources available to those searching for help.

Our mission has always focused on helping people flourish. In an ever-changing world with mixed messages, confused priorities, and flawed models, it is increasingly difficult to find inspiration and accompaniment grounded in timeless Gospel truth. We aim to be that accompaniment and are obsessed with remaining true to authentic principles of human identity.

Proceeds from The CatholicPsych Press go to serve the work of The CatholicPsych Foundation, a 501c3 public charity. The Foundation serves to meet material needs of many living in poverty in Haiti, recognizing that we cannot approach emotional wellbeing without first providing basic physical needs like food and shelter. It also provides mental health services to priests, religious, missionaries, and those in financial distress. Lastly, we provide equitable opportunities for authors to bring their story to life with an innovative model of equal partnership and sharing net revenue.

The book you hold in your hand was selected because of our confidence that it will move the needle forward in the lives of many people who earnestly desire to become whole, happy, and healthy - the saints they were created to be. This is the goal of the CatholicPsych Press, and we hope and pray that this work will bless you and be a source of renewal for your life.

Dr. Gregory Bottaro,
Executive Director of The CatholicPsych Institute